RUNNING ON EMPTY

Running on Empty

Refilling Your Spirit at the Low Points of Life

Jill Briscoe

Harold Shaw Publishers
Wheaton, Illinois

Unless otherwise noted, Scripture quotations are taken from *The Holy Bible, New International Version.* Copyright © 1973, 1978, 1984 International Bible Society. Used by permission of Zondervan Publishing House. All rights reserved.

Scriptures marked KJV are taken from the King James Version.

ISBN 0-87788-739-X

Cover design by David LaPlaca

Library of Congress Cataloging-in-Publication Data

Briscoe, Jill.
    Running on empty / Jill Briscoe.
      p. cm.
    Originally published: Dallas : Word Pub., © 1988.
    ISBN 0-87788-739-X (pbk.)
    1. Spiritual life—Christianity. 2. Bible—Biography. I. Title.
BV4501.2.B743 1995
248.4—dc20   95-23588
                                                         CIP

---

02 01 00 99 98 97 96 95

10 9 8 7 6 5 4 3 2 1

To my favorite preacher, Stuart

God's choice servant, and my beloved husband,
who for so many years has been faithful
in seeing to it that he has been running on full,
that he may be the means of breaking the bread of life
small enough for me to grasp, cutting it up in bite-sized
pieces and presenting it in such a way that it has been
all joy to be so nourished!

Thank you that my heart has grown fat,
and my soul's deepest needs have been abundantly met.

Contents

Introduction

Have you ever felt as if you were running on empty? I have, and for all sorts of reasons. The daily drama of living in an "ordinary" family, or the too-frequent trauma of coping with a fractured family, can find us spent before the day is through. Those in ministry who are supposed to be "a blessing" every day, or those trying to "do" something in un-doable church situations know full well how it is to find the "full well" empty! What a relief then to discover the "greats" of the Bible running on empty on occasion!

There was Elijah, flat on his face under the broom tree wanting to die; and Jonah, mad enough with God to kill himself. There was Leah, hating herself for being ugly and unloved; and Hannah, living with her broken dreams. And even King David felt fifty and fretful.

How did they get into their various stages of exhaustion, doubt, despair, and suicidal depression? More important, how did the God of fullness fill them up at the point of their deepest need?

It is because I want to love God supremely and serve him appropriately and believe you want to, too, that I have sought answers from the Scriptures and have written this book. May you find him filling all the empty places in your life in the days to come.

Jill Briscoe

Running on Empty

If I'm running on empty in my Christian life,
If I yell at my kids, if I put down my wife,
If my home is a mess and I'm down in
   the dumps,
I've got a good case of the spiritual mumps!

If I'm running on empty, burnt out and sad,
If I'm feeling rejected, frustrated, and mad,
If I'm angry that God hasn't answered
   my prayers,
That he's left me to carry my problems and
   cares . . .

Then I need to stay still and stop running away
From his cool Word of peace in the heat of
   the day.
If I'd open my heart to the Spirit's control
It wouldn't take long till the Lord filled my soul!

1

Elijah

Burnout

Now Ahab told Jezebel everything Elijah had done and how he had killed all the prophets with the sword. So Jezebel sent a messenger to Elijah to say, "May the gods deal with me, be it ever so severely, if by this time tomorrow I do not make your life like that of one of them."

Elijah was afraid and ran for his life. When he came to Beersheba in Judah, he left his servant there, while he himself went a day's journey into the desert. He came to a broom tree, sat down under it and prayed that he might die. "I have had enough, Lord," he said. "Take my life; I am no better than my ancestors." Then he lay down under the tree and fell asleep.

All at once an angel touched him and said, "Get up and eat." He looked around, and there by his head was a cake of bread baked over the hot coals, and a jar of water. He ate and drank and then lay down again.

The angel of the Lord came back a second time and touched him and said, "Get up and eat, for the journey is too much for you." So he got up and ate and drank. Strengthened by that food, he traveled forty days and forty nights until he reached Horeb, the mountain of God. There he went into a cave and spent the night.

1 Kings 19:1-9

ave you ever felt like a pooped prophet? Perhaps you have been diligently serving the Lord, but just doing too much of everything—running round and round in circles, until eventually you've met yourself coming back. Suddenly it all overwhelms you. If this is the case, watch out! You could end up flat on your face under a broom tree, just like Elijah.

It is one thing to be tired "in" the work of the Lord; it is quite another to be tired "of" the work itself. There is a difference, you know. When Elijah said, "I've had it, Lord," he meant it! He was tired of all of it.

Occasionally my husband, Stuart, wakes up in the morning and says, "I was born tired, I've lived tired, and I'll probably die tired!" This doesn't mean he is tired of his work; it simply means he's tired in the midst of it. And given the odds stacked against him, that's probably how it's going to be for the rest of his life!

So the question is: how can we live tired and live well, so we don't end up running on empty? I think our friend Elijah can help us.

What a colorful character Elijah was! He arrived on the stage of history in dramatic fashion and exited even more dramatically. In between those two events, he was a significant spiritual voice in his quiet, sad world of drought and death.

Ahab—otherwise known as Old King Compromise—was ruling Israel at that time. Thinking it prudent to make an alliance with the powerful nations around him, he married Jezebel, daughter of a heathen king. Ahab did this, of course, in direct disobedience to God's commandment that the Israelites stay separate from such entanglements. In fact, the Bible says that Ahab did more "to provoke the

Lord, the God of Israel, to anger than did all the kings of Israel before him" (1 Kings 16:33).

Apparently Jezebel came into Ahab's house quietly enough at first. But there was one thing Ahab had not bargained for: along with Jezebel came her pagan religion of Baal worship. In essence she said, "Take me—take my gods!" Believing Baal to be far more vigorous and powerful a god than El—the God of the Israelites—she told Ahab that his troubles stemmed from worshiping the wrong deity.

Jezebel and her people believed Baal to be the god of rain and fire, and it wasn't long before the queen made her beliefs influence the land. King Ahab set up altars for Baal, and many Israelites (including some of the prophets) began to worship this false god, while others were confused and puzzled by these happenings. In those days few of the Lord's prophets were prepared to take on the hierarchy. Jezebel had, in fact, been persecuting the sons of the prophets, and it was far too dangerous to publicly take Jehovah's side. Obadiah, a high official who was a secret believer, had been spiriting away the prophets and hiding them in caves at great personal risk (1 Kings 18:4). But apart from this act of courage, only Elijah stood up to Ahab.

Prophets are usually not known for their tact, and Elijah was no exception. Ahab had been out looking for pasture for his dying cattle when Elijah suddenly appeared on the scene. "You think things are bad now," Elijah said. "Just wait!"

Elijah's very name proclaimed to the world whose he was and whom he served: *El*, meaning "the Creator, the omnipotent God," and *jah*, meaning "coming from Jehovah—" the Lord's personal name. It could not fail to remind Ahab of the Lord's power. Elijah informed Ahab there would be no rain whatsoever (not even dew) for the next few years, except at his order. God had shut up the heavens at Elijah's request! Now they would all see who was the God of thunder and lightning and rain!

It is James, in the New Testament, who tells us about the prayer life of Elijah and explains how the powerful and effective petitions of this one man caused God to lock the rain in the rooms of heaven and seal the windows tight (James 5:17-18). Oh, for a prayer life of such effectiveness! If we knelt and asked God to bring faith to the heart of a faithless partner, or healing to a sick parent, or safety to a teenager in moral danger, could we tell the world of such answers as Elijah's?

And yet the Bible says "Elijah was a man just like us" (James 5:17). Yes, it really says that! However strong he might appear, Elijah was not a perfect man. (There was only One of those, and his name was not Elijah.) The prophet had learned to pray the hard way—without seminars, books, and video cassettes. He had known adversity, danger, and loneliness. The situations in which he found himself were so often beyond his control that they demanded his complete dependence upon God.

It's hard for a strong person to learn to depend. No one likes to lose control, especially a strong man. This was illustrated for me vividly when I was on a flight to Denver, Colorado. During the flight, the weather deteriorated until we were being tossed around quite violently. The young man next to me was really nervous. "I don't like it when I'm not in control," he said. "I'm a strong man—I don't let others rule my destiny. This makes me frightened." Actually I thought he was being strong in admitting his fear, and I told him that sometimes it takes strong situations to turn strong people into dependent ones.

Look at Elijah—surely he is one of the strongest figures in the Old Testament—yet in the space of a few short pages, we see him having to depend on birds to feed him and a widow to hide him. He stood alone on Carmel, and when he ran to Jezreel, he could depend on no one but his one humble servant. It's in such extremity of spirit that dependence is nurtured, faith is matured, and fervent prayer fostered. There was nothing the matter with Elijah's prayer life. And if our prayers are to accomplish much, we mustn't be surprised to find ourselves, like Elijah, enrolled in the school of hard knocks!

So if Elijah was such a holy man—praying up a storm (or down a storm), fighting spiritual lethargy, confronting Israel's king with his sin, and generally rushing about the world being a mighty model of a man—whatever happened to him? How did he end up under a broom tree, crying out, "I've had enough, Lord"?

If you take time to read the span of Scripture that journals Elijah's life and doings, I think you'll find there was nothing wrong with his relationship with the Lord up to this moment of deep need. In fact, everything was gloriously right up to this point. For three long years there had not been one drop of rain, just as Elijah had promised Ahab. God Himself had kept Elijah safe, leading him to refuge by a brook and sending ravens to feed him. Then God allowed the brook to dry up! What a test of Elijah's faith. Have you ever been certain you have done the right thing and then found that the brook had dried up on you? How did you react? With fortitude or panic? Apparently Elijah passed that test of faith, too.

Then God gave Elijah some companionship. (It's lonely being a prophet preaching an unwelcome message!) He sent Elijah to the town of Zarephath where a widow and her son cared for him. They shared their last meal with the hungry prophet—at least they thought it was their last meal. But God miraculously kept the food coming through long months of drought and famine. At last it was time. God told Elijah to face Ahab again.

On the Lord's behalf, Elijah summoned the nation of Israel and the prophets of Baal to a contest at which he intended to show who—El or Baal—was the one true God. Having proven Elohim was the God of rain, Elijah now determined to prove that he was also the master of fire.

The people assembled at the foot of Mount Carmel and followed Elijah up to the top, where he and the prophets of Baal proceeded to build their respective altars on which sacrifices were to be offered. Elijah, wanting to prove his point beyond doubt, ordered his offering to be drenched with water. Since this probably had to be hauled all the way from the foot of the mountain, there must have been little doubt in the minds of the Israelites doing all that donkey work that it would be a powerful God indeed who could send fire to consume such a soggy sacrificial mess!

After the prophets of Baal had finished leaping and prancing about and cutting themselves with knives (as was their custom in worship), and had received absolutely no answers from their god, Elijah called on his God. "O Lord, God of Abraham, Isaac and Israel, let it be known today that you are God in Israel and that I am your servant and have done all these things at your command. Answer me, O Lord, answer me, so these people will know that you, O Lord, are God, and that you are turning their hearts back again" (1 Kings 18:36-37).

"Then," the Bible simply says, "the fire of the Lord fell" (1 Kings 18:38). Oh, to have been there! To have seen a man pray prayers of such power and might that fire was obedient and rain began its hard work after its long holiday in heaven! No, there was nothing wrong with Elijah's faith at this point as far as I can see. So why, oh why, do we find him flat on his face under a broom tree crying, "I've had enough, Lord"?

Perhaps the clue lies in the intervening verses. After pleading with God for the long-awaited rain, Elijah saw the cloud of God's blessing advancing on the horizon (1 Kings 18:44). Delighted, he ran down the mountain and informed Ahab who was sitting in his chariot, probably scared to death to go home and face his wife. After all, Elijah had just summarily dispatched 450 of her prophets. Elijah told the king to hurry as the rains were on the way and he wouldn't want his chariot wheels to get stuck in the mud! Then, Elijah ran in front of the chariot all the way to the gates of Jezreel. (This, incidentally, was no mere stone's throw, but rather twenty-three hard miles.)

It's at this point that I first began to conclude that Elijah had a type A personality! Notice that he ran in front of the chariot, not behind it. Why didn't he accept a ride—assuming Ahab offered him one? Probably because an Elijah person always runs when he could easily walk or ride.

Are you an Elijah person? Do you go from one event to the next in grand style, shaking your fist at the devil, laughing at Jezebel and her prophets, taking on Ahab? Do you do it all until all you do finishes you off? Until, like God's prophet, you end up lying under a broom tree, suddenly tired *of* the work, rather than tired *in* it? Are you saying even as you read this, "I've had enough, Lord! I'm running on empty"?

Elijah was met at the gates of the city by a messenger from Jezebel who said to him, "May the gods deal with me, be it ever so severely, if by this time tomorrow I do not make your life like that of one of [the beheaded prophets of Baal]" (1 Kings 19:2). Then we read some startling words, for the record says, "Elijah was afraid"! AFRAID! How can this be? The man who had been afraid of no one? And then it says he "ran for his life" (19:3). The man who had feared only God, and kept his commandments turned tail and ran away from the will of God!

Have you ever wondered if God was disappointed at that moment? To have Elijah in town, Jezebel beaten, and Israel ready to do business with him—and then to have Elijah head off in the wrong direction would certainly have finished us off if we were God. But God is not like us—and aren't you glad about that? Knowing everything in advance, he had made provision. Around the corner of the desert, waiting for Elijah, was a broom tree!

Elijah had left his servant behind at Beersheba. We are not told why. Perhaps the poor man was lying under a broom tree of his own! After all, he had been at Elijah's side through thick and thin, and in all probability had "had it too, Lord!" Maybe Elijah had left his servant behind because he felt it would be a bad witness to the young man if he saw the prophet depressed. Or maybe Elijah wanted to isolate himself, as many of us tend to do when we are down. The last thing we want is an audience when we are feeling overcome.

If I am out of sorts with everyone, I don't need to be around anyone who is in sorts with everyone. That only serves to make me feel even more uncomfortable about my own attitude. And yet that is the time I really need someone around to help me. If we could only learn not to isolate ourselves in times of deep trouble, we would receive ministry to our wounded spirits that would bless not only us but also those who minister to us. But type A personalities have a hard time receiving; they are used to giving. Those who are in positions of authority and responsibility are used to having others look to them for strength; they have a hard time looking to others for help.

What was it Jesus told us to do? Wasn't it to get into our "closet" alone and meet with the Father? Well, here was Elijah, then, alone in his desert broom closet. And who should meet him there but the angel of the Lord, who had been busy—cooking breakfast! "A cake of bread baked over hot coals" (1 Kings 19:6). What a practical gift of love!

Many a time when I have been flat on my face under my own broom tree, God has sent some practical expression of love to remind me that he cares. I have eaten not a few hot cakes from the hand of God in my time.

Once when this happened I had been traveling for two weeks straight, speaking at meetings. Somehow the tight schedule allowed only time for talking and not much for eating! Whenever it was mealtime, I found myself on one more airplane. On this particular day it was hot, it was summer, and I was tired and hungry. My flight had been delayed, and by the time I arrived at the next conference center, I discovered that my hosts had gone to bed. (In the morning I learned that because of the delayed flight, they presumed I would not be coming until the following day—hence, no welcoming committee.) I wandered around the large dining room, hoping to find something to eat, but all the doors into the kitchen had been locked. "Lord," I prayed, "I really don't care what I eat, but I need something—and while I'm talking to you about this, I've got a yearning for peaches! Oh, for a lovely, refreshing, juicy peach!" Then I smiled. That was just the sort of prayer I counseled others against offering! I sighed, picked up my bags, and went to my assigned cabin.

When I arrived at my room, there were my hot cakes baked on the coals! A basket of peaches sat on the doorstep smiling up at me! I lifted them up and felt my loving Lord's smile. (It could have been oranges and apples, you know!) Never before or since have I received a whole basket of delicious, fresh peaches. But he who was waiting round the corner of my desert met and provided a sweet touch that reminded me of his great love.

When you find yourself exhausted, burned out—look around for the hot cakes. If you take time, you'll smell the bread and be reminded of God's care by some practical expression of concern through one of his children.

Notice, God did not feed his exhausted servant bitter herbs in order to punish him. He did not beat the already beaten man with a ministry stick and shout, "On your feet, you stupid coward, and share the four spiritual laws with Jezebel." The Bible simply says that God touched Elijah with the loving words, "Get up and eat, for the journey is too much for you" (1 Kings 19:7).

When I lose my perspective on life because I'm running on empty, I can soon lose my perspective on God himself. I need to be still and feel his loving touch and hear him say to me, "Go to sleep, rest awhile; the journey is too great for you." I am the sort of person who always seems to need permission to go to sleep—to relax, to walk the fields, smell the flowers, or recuperate. So, unless "have fun" is entered on my weekly schedule, I'll never have it!

Does that sound familiar? Has the journey suddenly become too great for you—not because everything is all wrong with your relationship with God, but because everything has been all right and you've simply run yourself into the ground? What swept you off your feet and sent you hurrying away from your responsibilities? Actually, it matters not what caused the changes, but only *Who* waits for you with hot cakes and cool water for your hungry, thirsty soul, assuring you of his love and great concern for your well-being.

Notice, too, that at this point the Lord's answer to Elijah's dilemma was a physical one. My own tendency is to open my Bible at such times and begin feverishly skimming the Scriptures for a cup of spiritual cream! If the Lord gets my ear, I'm often amazed to hear him say to me, "Put away your Bible and go to sleep! We'll talk about this in the morning!" We need to be careful not to look only for spiritual answers to physical problems!

Twice God touched Elijah and told him to sleep and take his rest while he stood guard over his spent child. What a help it is at such times to think of the verse that says, "He who watches over Israel will neither slumber nor sleep" (Ps. 121:4). After all, there is no point in both of us staying awake!

God had been equal to Elijah's past and would be equal to Elijah's needs in the future too. It was Elijah's present that was the problem! But doesn't the Bible say that Jesus Christ is the same yesterday, today, and forever (Heb. 13:8)? Like Elijah, many Christians can say Jesus has been sufficient in their past, forgiving them and making them his children. And of course they know he will be there in heaven to welcome them home. But it's the present problems that bring them to their broom closets!

So in the morning Elijah woke up and turned his face toward Horeb, the mountain of God. I've asked myself many times, "Why Horeb?" Surely there were other vacation spots more accessible.(After all, it took him forty days and forty nights to get there!) This is one of those questions the Bible doesn't answer, but if we peek around the corner of a verse, we'll be delighted and surprised by the people we find in the shadows, the color of the clouds, or the discovery of an orchid flowering on a garbage pile! So let's peek.

Perhaps Elijah went to Horeb to get back to his spiritual roots. That's always a good thing to do. It's what we have known of God's faithfulness in the past that will encourage us to have faith for the present. When we are down, we can be helped up by remembering God's dealings with people like us: men and women in the Scriptures. And wasn't it at Horeb that Moses—living in the back side of the desert, a fugitive from Pharaoh and a murderer to boot—heard the angel of the Lord assure him of God's hand upon his life? Wasn't it at Horeb that water sprang from the rock to quench the thirst of the children of Israel? And wasn't it at Horeb, the place of Israel's greatest treachery—the worship of the golden calf—that God dealt with their sin and sent the people on their way toward Canaan? Is failure ever final for God's children? No!

Perhaps Elijah needed to think about this heritage and that is why he went to Horeb. But, no matter why he went, Elijah found—as Moses had before him—that the desert was not silent. God can speak from any old bush or in any deep cave. We cannot stop the insistent, persistent voice of the Spirit who wills us to listen and learn from the very heart of God.

I think, however, that Elijah did try to stop hearing God's voice, for he wrapped his cloak around his ears (1 Kings 19:13). After allowing the prophet time to recoup and regroup, the angel of the Lord asked, "What are you doing here, Elijah?" (If we take ourselves out of ministry, God will always want to know why. Not that he is ignorant of the reasons of course, but his questions require an answer from us, and answers require reasons for our position.)

"I have been very zealous for the Lord God Almighty. The Israelites have rejected your covenant, broken down your altars, and put your prophets to death with the sword. I am the only one left, and now they are trying to kill me too," Elijah complained (1 Kings 19:14).

Isn't it funny how we harp on one theme when we get down? We get a bee in our bonnet about something someone has said or hasn't said. Some lack of caring on the part of a church member, or the fact that no one came to visit us when we asked for help. And if we are not careful, we get mud on our glasses and see everyone and everything in a murky hue.

So it was with Elijah. His resentment about Israel boiled and boiled. "Where were they when I stood up to be counted?" he demanded. "Why didn't they stand up to

Jezebel?" he complained bitterly. "There's not a spiritual one among the lot of them. I am the only one left."

Then the Lord spoiled Elijah's pity party with the sharp reminder that there were actually seven thousand Israelites just like him—seven thousand who "have not bowed down to Baal" (1 Kings 19:18). God made it clear that it was not time yet for Elijah to hole up in a holy hill of retirement! There was work to be done that only he could do.

How self-righteous we can get when we are wounded, and yet self-righteousness has never helped the healing process. There's work to be done that will never get done if we retire to lick our real or imaginary wounds—caused by our condemning others for their real or imaginary faults.

God asked Elijah, "What are YOU doing?" not "What are *they* doing?" The implication was, "Focus on your own calling, and leave me to judge your brothers."

Duly rebuked, Elijah was ready for his marching orders: "Go back the way you came," said the Lord (1 Kings 19:15). And Elijah went!

The rest of Elijah's wonderful story continues as you might expect—with lots of whirlwind activity, mighty living, and holy talking! When it's finished, God honors him with a very special death and sends the heavenly limousine right to the door for him! What an exit! And yet, the lasting picture in my mind is not the man swept up into heaven in a fiery chariot, but the crumpled shape of the dispirited man lying under the broom tree. I'm reminded that though he'd "had it" with the Lord's work, the Lord had not had it with him! And he has not had it with us either. He is intent on renewing, refreshing, and refilling us until our work is done!

Yesterday He walked with me
> through fields of sunlight,
helping me pick
> the fresh flowers of faith.

Today He promises He will be
all that I need
> as the occasion arises.

And now I can walk
> around the corner of tomorrow,
knowing He'll be there
> just as He was in all my yesterdays,
for
> JESUS IS THE SAME!

Refueling

Responding to the Chapter:
A Guide for Individuals and Groups

---

1. What is the significance of these names?
   - (a) Baal
   - (b) Elijah

---

2. Why did God consider Ahab an evil king (see 1 Kings 16)?

---

3. How does your prayer life compare with Elijah's? Read James 5:16-18 and 1 Kings 18:41-45.

---

4. Take each passage and glean the most meaningful thought from it.
   - (a) 1 Kings 17:1-5
   - (b) 1 Kings 17:7-24
   - (c) 1 Kings 18:1-15
   - (d) 1 Kings 18:16-40

---

5. Read 1 Kings 19:1-18.
   - (a) How does God deal with Elijah?
   - (b) What can we learn from the way God helped someone who was depressed?
   - (c) What does Elijah do to help himself?

Prayer Time

Pray for people you know who struggle with things as Elijah did. Pray for the Elijah-like patterns you see in yourself.

2

Leah

Rejection

Now Laban had two daughters; the name of the older was Leah, and the name of the younger was Rachel. Leah had weak eyes, but Rachel was lovely in form, and beautiful. Jacob was in love with Rachel and said, "I'll work for you seven years in return for your younger daughter Rachel."

Laban said, "It's better that I give her to you than to some other man. Stay here with me." So Jacob served seven years to get Rachel, but they seemed like only a few days to him because of his love for her.

Then Jacob said to Laban, "Give me my wife. My time is completed, and I want to lie with her."

So Laban brought together all the people of the place and gave a feast. But when evening came, he took his daughter Leah and gave her to Jacob . . .

When morning came, there was Leah! So Jacob said to Laban, "What is this you have done to me? I served you for Rachel, didn't I? Why have you deceived me?"

Genesis 29:16-23, 25

She was older than her sister—and uglier. There was no use denying it. She had lived with it forever, or so it seemed. Every man around had eyes only for her sister Rachel, and the comparison cut like a knife into Leah's heart.

Even the obvious advantages of being born first appeared to be disadvantages, clouding her judgment, causing despair, and worse—spawning resentment, bitterness and jealousy. Such was Leah's case. And if she had any doubt as to her inferiority, she only had to think of their names: Rachel meant ewe, whereas Leah meant cow!

One wonders if the two sisters had ever loved each other. Certainly the Bible gives no indication that they had. But then we meet them after they are full-grown and already victims, caught up in a web of intrigue woven by their crafty father. By the time we are introduced to Leah and Rachel, they have plenty of reasons to hate each other.

And then along came the handsome stranger, Jacob. And it wasn't enough that every man in the neighborhood wanted Rachel; Jacob wanted her too—enough to ask for her hand in marriage and serve Laban seven years to get her. Now Leah, the eldest, would not even be given in marriage first. What shame!

Then, finally, her scheming father gave her the advantage. He came to her tent door with a plan that was to his benefit, but, as he pointed out to Leah, would also give her a husband—and a desirable one at that.

However sorry we feel for Leah, we have to realize that she was apparently willing to go along with her father's deception—and an incredible deception it turned out to be. Laban suggested that Leah pretend to be her younger sister, not revealing herself until the light of day when the elaborate wedding ceremony was over and the marriage consummated. Only when it was too late would Jacob discover himself married to the wrong woman. Did Leah think, perhaps, better the wrong man than no man at all?

"When morning came, there was Leah," the Bible cryptically states. From our vantage point it seems weird that Jacob didn't realize his wife's true identity until morning, but doubtless this had to do with the marriage customs of that day.

To give Jacob his due, at least he didn't divorce Leah. When people today find their marriages in trouble, they often say, in essence, "When morning came, there was Leah!" They tell me tales of expecting one thing and then waking up to reality. After looking at their partners in the clear light of day they say, "Oh, no! I never expected this!"

The next thing you know, they are talking about divorce. "It would be far better for all concerned," they say. And when you listen to their sad state of affairs, it's tempting to believe they are right. It's tempting also to believe it would have been better for Leah if the whole sad arrangement had finished as soon as it began. But Jacob didn't divorce Leah. Instead, he vented his fury on his father-in-law, demanding that Laban give him Rachel as he had promised.

It takes a twister to twist a twister, and there was certainly a smack of poetic justice about the whole thing. Jacob had cheated his brother Esau out of his birthright and had to run for his life because of it. Now he himself had been cheated out of his own prize—the beautiful young woman he loved.

At this point in the biblical narrative, Jacob's love for Rachel is the only redeeming part of the sordid story. There is something beautiful about the fact that for Jacob the seven years of hard labor "seemed like only a few days to him because of his love for her" (Gen. 29:20).

However, romantic though it might have been, this love only served to contrast the terrible hatred that was now turned upon Leah. And however much she may have deserved it, our hearts go out to Leah—locked into a loveless relationship, with no end to the bitterness, rejection, and hostility heaped upon her. For the Bible states very clearly that this was the case. Hated by her sister, rejected by her husband, and used by her father for his own sordid ends—is it any wonder Leah was running on empty?

But if the story begins badly, it gets worse. For the crafty Laban struck again, promising Jacob his heart's desire in return for seven more years of work. "It is not our custom here to give the younger daughter in marriage before the older one. Finish this daughter's bridal week; then we will give you the younger one also, in return for another seven years of work" (Gen. 29:26-27). So Jacob lived out the bridal week with Leah, and then Laban gave him Rachel "to be his wife" (Gen. 29:28).

I doubt that Leah's brief honeymoon week was one of nuptial bliss. And then to see the lovers united—to watch Jacob's total delight in her beautiful sister—must have cut like a knife into her rejected heart.

In her anguish and bitterness, Leah discovered a weapon with which to fight back. However beautiful her sister was on the outside, there was something drastically wrong on the inside. Rachel could not conceive! And Jacob, desiring children, was not above using Leah's body for a night to achieve his ends.

"Surely my husband will love me now," Leah said wistfully, pathetically. It was not the first time, nor would it be the last, that a baby has been used as a weapon in the battle of human relationships!

It is difficult for us to tell how well Leah knew the Lord, although we can certainly see God's concern for her.

"When the Lord saw that Leah was not loved, he opened her womb" (Gen. 29:31). "The Lord saw," the Scripture says. But he did more than that: he acted on Leah's behalf. Even though she had been foolish and deceitful, he sent someone to alleviate her misery.

He does the same for Leahs today, and many times the someone he sends is a child. Children are to mothers as wing is to bird, rain is to cloud. When you are living with daily rejection, God can reveal himself to you in many ways, not the least of which is through your relationship with children.

And strangely enough, even though Leah's fertility began a sad saga of doing everything she could to get her husband to sleep with her, including bribing her sister for the privilege, it also reveals a growing relationship with her God. The names of Leah's children tell us a great deal about her spiritual journey.

Hebrew names have great significance. They are a revelation of character—both of the bearer of the name and the giver. Reuben was Leah's firstborn son, and his name, which sounds like the Hebrew words "The Lord has seen my misery," actually meant "See, a son." Apparently, the birth of her first son reminded Leah that God was not blind to her needs. He had "seen" her deep misery and had sent her a blessing.

The hardest thing to believe when you are suffering rejection is that anyone is noticing you at all. Misery makes us miserable, and though the old adage says misery loves company, company usually doesn't love misery. Not too many people seek out the weepers and the wailers of the world. It's harder still to believe God is interested in our misery. We cannot see him, and circumstances seem to underline his absence. We need a Reuben in our lives! We need to be reminded, in some shape or size, that the "Lord has seen our misery!"

Evidences of God's benevolence can be found in many forms. Perhaps your husband has indeed rejected you; like Leah, you are left in little doubt that the "other woman" is loved and you are not. But what about your children, or your parents, your sisters or brothers, or your good friends? Perhaps Reuben has been there all along, but because of your preoccupation with your troubles you have not even realized it.

Simeon was born next, and his name meant "one who hears." Perhaps Leah thought that along with seeing her misery, God also heard her prayers. "Because the Lord heard that I am not loved," she said, "he gave me this one too" (Gen. 29:33).

Leah was beginning to recognize God's concern for her in practical terms. The Lord provided her with companionship when her husband was no companion, love when her husband was no lover, and friendship when her husband was no friend. He had given her the caring beyond her husband: the love, companionship, and friendship of her children.

I hear some of you say, "But I have not been rejected by a husband—I do not have a husband at all! And I do not have any children. Ask me what that feels like! *That's* rejection."

I have a very dear friend who has never married, though she has had the chance. However, in the course of her work, she has given her love to hundreds of children. One day she said to me, "I am so rich! Here I am—not married, but I count myself to have hundreds and hundreds of children. 'Because more are the children of the desolate woman than of her who has a husband.' How much I have!" And she began to talk of her "Reubens" and "Simeons" as if they were literally her own.

I have another friend who counts her "aunthood" a sacred gift of happiness and enjoys it with as much joy as

I have seen—yes, even more joy than I have seen many mothers exhibit!

The third son Leah bore to Jacob was named Levi. Levi sounds like, and may have been derived from, the Hebrew word for "attached." At his birth Leah said, "Now at last my husband will become attached to me, because I have borne him three sons. So he was named Levi" (Gen. 29:34). What hopes poor Leah had. And how some of us can identify with this. When we are out of favor with a husband, a child, a parent, or a friend, what lengths we will go to to fix that attachment. The mother of a hostile teenager will buy her pouting daughter a dress she really cannot afford in order that her estranged child will become "attached" to her. A husband sensing his wife's coldness toward him may desperately try to please her in order to ignite the flames of love again. And occasionally, a girl will make sure she gets pregnant in order to "compel" love!

Alas, Leah's three sons had seemingly no effect upon Jacob where his attachment to her was concerned. Somewhere between verse 34 and 35, however, Leah must have found a measure of peace in her children. For when her fourth child was born, she named him Judah, which may have been derived from the Hebrew word for "praise." She said, "This time I will praise the Lord."

If only we can get to this point and be able to say, "Though my husband does not love me, the Lord does, and I will praise him for the blessings I *do* have." Then a measure of peace will be found. When you are rejected, running on empty, praise is a powerful refueling agent!

Leah's peace of mind didn't last long, however. Having wrestled with her husband's rejection even after bearing him his first four sons, she now faced the hostility and envy of her beautiful and favored sister. For Rachel, we are told, became jealous of her sister because Leah had children and she had none (Gen. 30:1).

One has to feel sorry for Rachel, too. After all, Jacob had been her promised husband. She had waited patiently for him for seven long years. Then her father and sister had tricked her on her wedding night! How would you or I have felt about that? And along with all this, she found she couldn't get pregnant. And in Rachel's time there was far more at stake in that than the thought of not having a family; to be barren was considered a sign of divine disfavor. Now she feared God was denying her a family! Why did God favor Leah and not her? she wondered.

Yes, the beautiful and loved Rachel was struggling with rejection too. And what rejection! The thought that God had bypassed her for another had to feel like *total* rejection. The fear that she was not good enough for God, or not fit to be trusted with children, must have haunted and taunted Rachel. Eventually it led to her frantic, unfair demand of Jacob: "Give me children, or I'll die! (Gen. 30:1)." Tragically, Rachel did die—not because God withheld children, but because he gave them! I am reminded of the verse that says, "So he gave them what they asked for, but sent a wasting disease upon them" (Ps. 106:15). To hammer on the door of heaven long enough may mean you will beat the door down one day and end up flat on your face with a broken neck!

Jacob's angry response didn't help much either. "Am I in the place of God, who has kept you from having children?" he asked (Gen. 30:2). Now Rachel could do without that. Not only was Jacob upset with her, but he was more or less saying that God was too.

Finding her fists red and raw from battering on doors that wouldn't open, Rachel resorted to plan B. She would have children one way or another—whatever the cost. So she gave her servant Bilhah to Jacob as his concubine, and Bilhah bore Jacob two sons. Rachel named them Dan, meaning "vindicated," and Naphtali, meaning "my struggle." She said, "God has vindicated me," and "I have had a great struggle with my sister, and I have won" (Gen. 30:6, 8).

Poor Bilhah! Who ever gave her a second thought? Not Rachel—or Leah, or, we suspect, Jacob. What rejection she must have suffered. And she was not alone. Leah's hapless maid Zilpah was used in the same manner—a pawn in the sisters' game to win Jacob's attention. Zilpah produced two more sons for Jacob, and Leah called them Gad, "what good fortune," and Asher, "happy." But Leah's happiness, such as it was, was purchased at the price of another woman's unhappiness, and that sort of happiness never lasts long.

The years passed, and Jacob's sons grew. One day the eldest, Reuben, went into the fields and found some mandrake plants, which were superstitiously believed to induce pregnancy. So Rachel asked her sister, "Please give me some of your son's mandrakes" (Gen. 30:14). After all that happened, Rachel still persisted in somehow, some way, making sure she got what she wanted—even if it meant resorting to superstition. It's amazing to what lengths we will go to get our own way!

Leah's bitter response tells us that there was still no love lost between the sisters. "Wasn't it enough," she snapped, "that you took my husband? Will you take my son's mandrakes too?" (Gen. 30:15). Leah in her unhappiness and bitterness had forgotten that Jacob was really Rachel's husband in the first place! It's interesting how the memory plays tricks with the facts when you are unhappy. Leah only saw her side of the story.

Since there are always two ways of looking at things, it's so easy to take sides. All of us do it.

I remember our daughter calling me at one o'clock in the morning to tell me she had had a fight with her husband of two months. Everything in me wanted to run down the phone line, snatch my little girl away from this man who was daring to hurt her, and carry her off to safety. But I remembered I had told her that the Bible says you leave and cleave! I also remembered I had told her that once she was married, she must work out her problems with her husband, not with anyone else. So summoning all my willpower, I asked her, "Does Greg know you are calling me? Because if he doesn't, I won't talk to you!" "Greg *told* me to call you," she sobbed. "He said, 'I can't do anything with you; maybe your mother knows what's the matter with you!'" It's so easy to take sides. There I was ready to murder my poor son-in-law, and it had been he who had turned to me for help!

Rachel and Leah both had a cause to present. Both were struggling with pain and rejection. Rejection doesn't help you to be very objective. In fact, most of the time living with rejection leads to a pretty subjective view of things— leaves you reacting purely on an emotional level, which leads you to do things that in your better moments you would probably be thoroughly ashamed of doing.

Look at Rachel's answer to Leah's bitter accusation. "Very well," Rachel said, "[Jacob] can sleep with you tonight in return for your son's mandrakes" (Gen. 30:15). She was bartering sex for mandrakes. And listen to Leah, running to meet Jacob as he came in from the fields, blurting out, "You must sleep with me. I have hired you with my son's mandrakes" (30:16). And finally, look at Jacob's response, "So he slept with her that night" (30:16). Once things get to this level, apparently anything goes.

There is an interesting sidelight on Leah's character here. We hear her talking to herself because her "hired sex" resulted in one more baby named Issachar, which meant "reward." She said, "God has rewarded me for giving my maidservant to my husband" (30:17). Apparently she had been struggling with her own conscience, perhaps hating what she had done in her pathetic efforts to win her husband's attention. And God, the Bible says, "listened to Leah" (30:17).

Sometimes in our response to rejection, we find ourselves doing things we find difficult to live with afterward. Guilt compounds the problem. How can you feel good about yourself when you know you have used other people to your own selfish ends?

Yet however hurt she was, however guilty she felt, Leah never stopped talking to God. Her hurting heart didn't stop her, her guilt didn't stop her, her disappointment in herself didn't stop her. If the Bible says that God listened, then Leah must have kept on talking to him, and therein lay her salvation.

Despite this, Leah's lot in life never really changed. She had to learn to live with something she could never change.

Rejection in the short term is hard enough to cope with, but rejection over the long haul is a killer. To be able to sustain long-term rejection—to live with it day in and day out—necessitates lessons well-learned in the short term.

Though Rachel died in childbirth—the birth of her second son, Benjamin—Leah never replaced her sister in Jacob's affections. We don't know just when Leah died, but she may still have been living when her sons, wild men, sold Rachel's son Joseph—Jacob's favorite—into slavery, having narrowly been diverted from murdering him. If her children were a comfort to her when they were small, they don't sound like they were very good company once they were grown! Poor Leah!

Yet even though "poor Leah's" circumstances were trying beyond measure, God cared for her. He sustained her, watched out for her, and listened to her prayers.

There are many "poor Leahs" in this life. Perhaps you know such a person, or perhaps you are one yourself. We can learn much from Leah. We can learn that even when we face rejection, we must resist letting it turn us into its slave. We must refuse to obey its commands, refuse to sink to the depths it tempts us to.

Above all, remember that God alone knows what rejection is all about. He was rejected by the very world he made—his family, his friends, and his closest disciples. In our extreme pain we can lay our head on his breast and say, "You understand." He will succor us, fill us with the assurance of his sustaining presence, and enable us to keep on keeping on—though we be married to Jacob, have Rachel as our sister, and raise children like Reuben, Judah, and Levi. No matter how difficult our living situation, tomorrow is another day, and he has promised he will meet us around the corner of tomorrow with balm in his hands!

Refueling

---

1. Who do you feel the sorriest for—and why?
   - (a) Rachel
   - (b) Leah
   - (c) Bilhah and Zilpah
   - (d) Jacob
   - (e) the children

---

2 Read Isaiah 53.
   - (a) Which verse speaks the most graphically of the Lord's rejection?
   - (b) Which verse gives an example of handling rejection?

---

3. Think of ways you can help people suffering from rejection.

Prayer Time

Pray that the God of Jacob will remind you that he *is* the God of Jacob—and of Rachel, Laban, and Leah. He doesn't pick perfect people to bless with his presence, but people just like us.

3

David

Sin

Have mercy on me, O God,
  according to your unfailing love;
according to your great compassion
  blot out my transgressions. . . .

Cleanse me with hyssop, and I will be clean;
  wash me, and I will be whiter than snow.
Let me hear joy and gladness;
  let the bones you have crushed rejoice.
Hide your face from my sins
  and blot out all my iniquity.

Create in me a pure heart, O God,
  and renew a steadfast spirit within me.
Do not cast me from your presence
  or take your Holy Spirit from me.
Restore to me the joy of your salvation
  and grant me a willing spirit to sustain me.

Then I will teach transgressors your ways,
  and sinners will turn back to you.
Save me from bloodguilt, O God,
    the God who saves me,
    and my tongue will sing of your
      righteousness.
O Lord, open my lips,
  and my mouth will declare your praise.
You do not delight in sacrifice, or I would
    bring it;
    you do not take pleasure in burnt offerings.

The sacrifices of God are a broken spirit;
  a broken and contrite heart,
O God, you will not despise.

Psalm 51:1, 7-17

*I*n the spring a young man's fancy lightly turns to thoughts of love," the poet Tennyson wrote. And it certainly proved true where David was concerned. In fact, David had more than spring working against him. He was somewhere near fifty, and he was suddenly tired of fighting the battles of the Lord. You can almost hear him saying: "I've done my bit; let others do it now—younger ones, stronger ones—like Joab for instance." Joab was David's commanding officer. And so it was, "In the spring, at the time when kings go off to war, David sent Joab out with the king's men and the whole Israelite army. They destroyed the Ammonites and besieged Rabbah. But David remained in Jerusalem" (2 Sam. 11:1).

You could hardly blame David. He had been a warrior for so long, and had done so well. For years he had held God's name high and won the fight of faith. Starting way back with the giant Goliath, his record was impressive. His servants had often tried to restrain him from setting himself in the forefront of the battle. "The lamp of Israel must not be extinguished," they argued. Until this moment, war had been part of David's daily thoughts. But today was different. He was weary of the struggle—sluggish, suddenly fed up with the whole thing. So it was that David stayed at home, stayed in bed—and sent Joab.

David lived in a beautiful palace, with all the comforts a king would command. Seeing God gives us "all things richly to enjoy," who could blame David for enjoying all the rich things he'd been given? I'm sure he knew his palace must never become an end in itself, but maybe he was unaware that his lovely environment had become a snare to him. The fact remains, David's heart was a lot cleaner when he lived in a cave, hunted by Saul, than when he lived safe and secure in his castle! And isn't this often the case?

Can you relate to David? Are you tired of fighting the Lord's battles? Are you fifty and facing the inevitable slowing down process known as aging? Do you enjoy your pleasant home with its comfortable environment? Well, you are not alone!

I, too, can certainly relate to all of this. I am well-past fifty, and somehow this very fact has been a battle to battle! I have fought many a good fight in my years of Christian work. We have a lovely home too, and it isn't as easy as it used to be to leave with my little suitcase and go on the road, attending endless meetings, often arriving back home well past midnight, tired—welcomed only by a deserted, dark airport.

The last time I traveled, I "lost" my car in the multi-tiered car park at the airport in sub-zero weather. I remember saying to myself, "Who needs this? I certainly don't. I should stay home and send 'Joab' instead." But I knew I really don't have an option. I may be "king" in the sense that I can decide to do whatever I want, but I am forever servant to God, who calls and sends me. It is he who sets the battle, arrays me in his armor, and sends me out to fight the foe. I stay home at my peril if he has sent me forth.

There are concerns and temptations that can hit all of us at various stages and ages of life. And being older, one of the obvious ones is our physical state—the condition of our wonderful body "machine." Everything begins to loosen up and fall apart! A friend told me her favorite definition of old age: "When you bend down to fasten your shoelaces and think hard if there's anything else you can do while you're down there!"

There is, however, another temptation attached to middle age. Once you find yourself looking back on more than you are looking forward to, a certain amount of panic sets in. For a woman, the challenge becomes greater to look pretty, to stay trim, to care what people think when they look at you. "Am I still physically attractive to my husband or to men?" wonders a woman who has been endowed with good looks and is well aware that they are fading fast. For a man—a man like David—the same temptation was undoubtedly true. He had been a handsome young man who had a way with women, and now he was over fifty.

Thus the scene was set, and the devil took full advantage of David's vulnerability. Alone in the palace, morose, his troops out fighting his battles, David was ripe for the plucking. Perhaps he had been lying in bed feeling sorry for himself, thinking about all the glory past when he was young and virile. Whatever was in his mind, he couldn't sleep. So he got up and wandered out onto the rooftop of his Jerusalem palace. There, waiting for him, was temptation in the form of a beautiful woman.

We are not told how old Bathsheba was, but we are told she was "very beautiful." She was in her childbearing years and had a beautiful body, and David appreciated that!

Now, a word about temptation here. I have often heard my husband tell our teenagers, "Temptation is not only an opportunity to do the wrong thing, but an opportunity to do the right!" Although we usually consider temptation in negative terms, God allows us to be tempted in order to provide us with a chance to be obedient. If we are to learn to say no—and we are certainly supposed to say no sometimes to some things—then circumstances become life's workshop to that end. Saying no when you want to say yes strengthens you, produces endurance, and builds character—Christian character.

Another thing about temptation is that temptation in itself isn't sinful. It's "falling" into temptation that is.

Scripture says everyone is tempted and that there are common temptations that all of us experience (1 Cor. 10:12-13). Sexual temptations surely fall into that category. Confucius, a Chinese philosopher, said, "You can't stop the birds from flying over your head, but you can stop them from nesting in your hair!"

Unfortunately, David didn't take a brush and comb with him when he walked onto the rooftop that day. The first look wasn't sin, but the second was—and the third, and the fourth and the fifth! David, having seen the beautiful Bathsheba's body, decided to find out if being fifty mattered all that much. Apparently it didn't sexually, but it surely did spiritually! David, unfortunately, stayed far too long on the roof.

Have you ever been up on the rooftop with the birds fluttering over your head? What did you do about it? Did you come down in a hurry or allow them to nest in your hair?

I have a young friend—a mother of three—who needed to go back to work. Not long after she did so, her boss—a handsome, middle-aged, and charming man—let her know he wanted to entertain her in his "palace." The young woman fought a losing battle with temptation. She found she was not only flattered by all the attention, but began to dress in ways to fuel the flames. She stayed on the rooftop too long and disaster resulted.

At what point all this becomes sin, I'm not quite sure. Jesus said that adultery takes place in the mind first as far as God is concerned (Matt. 5:28). The problem for my friend was that she needed the job; her husband was out of work and they were in debt. It was not an easy thing for me to urge her to get herself another job. There were few to be found, and to look for other employment seemed to be running away instead of "overcoming" the temptation where she was. In this case, however, it was the only way she could save herself and her marriage. After falling into temptation, she repented, resigned, and within a week found another job; and eventually she was able to salvage some of her relationships.

I was speaking in Australia on this subject, and afterward a young and very pretty pastor's wife approached me.

"I would *never* commit adultery!" she said confidently.

"Never say never," I cautioned.

"Murder, yes," she laughed, "but never adultery!"

"Have you ever had the chance?" I inquired.

I was not surprised when she replied, "Yes," for she was very attractive.

"What happened?" I asked her.

"It was easy to say no," she replied.

"Let me ask you another question," I persisted. "Was the man who tempted you a 'King Lear' or a 'King David'?"

Suddenly she was not smiling. "A King Lear?" she said. "No." Then she said soberly, "I get your point. It's easy to say no to someone who's not all that attractive, but wait until I'm in a lonely spot and a King David comes along."

"Exactly," I said softly.

Our hearts are "deceitful above all things and beyond cure" (Jer. 17:9). We must never forget that.

Bathsheba's husband *was* out of town, and David *was* difficult to resist. From David's perspective, Bathsheba *was* very beautiful, and he *was* the king. And so the deed was done. Truly, these two traded a night of pleasure for a lifetime of pain. It doesn't take long to ruin your life, and David and Bathsheba soon found that the heady combination of laziness and loneliness spells big trouble!

The amazing thing to me isn't that two lonely people found each other in a moment of weakness, or even that the "man after God's own heart" continued in sin and hardened his heart to such a degree that he went on to murder Bathsheba's husband—who was, incidentally, one of his closest friends. No, the amazing thing is that for more than a year after all of this, David was running on empty and nobody knew it!

Well now, I suppose that's not really true. Joab knew it. At David's command he had set Uriah, Bathsheba's husband, into the front line of the fiercest part of the battle and then withdrawn support from him, exposing him to certain death. And God knew it! The Bible says God was "displeased" with David (2 Sam. 11:27). He was thoroughly upset with his servant.

David, however, either didn't know it, or didn't care. He continued singing psalms and dispensing advice, without ever repenting for what he had done. He was running on empty quite effectively. *That's* scary!

In the end, of course, the vehicle can't run on fumes and *does* come to a screeching halt. It's just a matter of time. In David's case, it was Nathan who threw up the roadblock.

David's friends are very interesting, for they played tremendously important roles in his life and development. His friend Jonathan, the son of Saul, loved David as his own soul. When David was on the run from Saul, he needed a friend. And to have Saul's own precious son become his closest friend was an incredible thing. And when Saul sought to end David's life, it was Jonathan who met him in the forest and "helped him find strength in God" (1 Sam. 23:16).

We all need a Jonathan in our lives, a friend who will stick with us through thick and thin and encourage us in God. A friend who will love us. But we also need a Nathan! Nathan wounded to heal. "Wounds from a friend can be trusted," so Proverbs tells us, and "iron sharpens iron" (Prov. 27:6, 17). And it was Nathan who faced David with the fact that he had been running on empty.

God's "Nathans" have a very special calling. They have the courage to take God's Word to friend and foe alike, however unpalatable it may be. Nathan certainly took his life in his hands when he faced King David with his sin. After all, David had sent Uriah to his death in order that his sin would not be discovered. It's humiliating to learn that others are fully aware of what you've done, especially when you are so sure you've covered your tracks!

A long time ago, I found my own heart growing bitter and resentful. I allowed my attitude toward the mission we served to deteriorate to such a degree that it was hard to be civil to anyone connected with it. I tried hard, however, not to allow my feelings to show. In fact, I began to be quite proud of the fact that I could fulfill my obligations to the mission while harboring all sorts of resentful thoughts, without anyone being aware of my condition. Once you've been in Christian circles long enough, it's comparatively easy to pull the wool over people's eyes. You just go through the motions, sing the hymns, pray the expected prayers, and smile the evangelical smile, and no one knows what you are really thinking—or so you come to believe!

Sitting smugly at the back of a meeting one night (you don't usually sit at the front if you're trying to duck the blessing), I was suddenly alerted by the preacher's words. "Some of you are bitter and resentful against the Lord's people," he said, "and you think no one knows how you feel."

"That's right," I said to myself. "No one knows my heart. I've become too good at putting on the act."

Having got my attention, the Holy Spirit lost no time directing "Nathan's" words in my direction. "The fact is," the preacher continued, "everyone knows you're empty. Because when there is no fullness of the Spirit in your life, no one receives the overflow! People are not getting any real spiritual blessing from you!"

I sat there stunned, until, like David, I was able to respond to that direct word from God, saying, "I have sinned! Forgive me, Lord." And, as he had with David, the Lord graciously heard me and answered my prayer.

If it is hard to listen to a Nathan, it is doubly hard to *be* one! It takes a brave person to be obedient to the Friend who "sticketh closer than a brother" (Prov. 18:24, KJV) but who we cannot see, when it involves a close brother or sister that we can see very well. But true friendship demands this kind of openness and honesty if it is to prosper.

So Nathan boldly faced David with his sin. "Why did you despise the word of the Lord by doing what is evil in his eyes?" he asked (2 Sam. 12:9). And David responded, rather than reacted, to the words of the prophet.

David composed a psalm about his repentance that gives us a wonderful pattern for renewal. It is Psalm 51. "Blot out my transgressions," David cried in verse 1. The image is that of a papyrus scroll on which God has recorded David's deeds, and as David takes a good hard look at the sin, the image on the papyrus, he seeks to have his sin erased. That is where we must start. As long as we refuse to take the blame, or blame others for our own wrongdoing, we'll never know God's renewal and restoring power. David could have said, "It's really not my fault, you know—it's Bathsheba's. Who could blame me when she threw herself at me in such a fashion!" Or he could have blamed his father. After all, he was always left out as a kid. Or then again, he could have accused his brothers who never accepted him. But he didn't do any of these things. He owned the sin himself—it was his alone—and began to talk to God about it.

Surely David realized he had hurt a lot of people with his sin. Yet in his confession he said, "Against you, you only, have I sinned and done what is evil in your sight" (Ps. 51:4). I think he addressed God in such a fashion because he knew that sin against anyone is a sin against God. Didn't Jesus say, "Whatever you did for one of the least of these brothers of mine, you did for me" (Matt. 25:40)? God is a holy, truthful, wise God, so anything unholy, devious, or stupid that we do to others offends the One who is holy and calls us to be likewise (Lev. 19:2).

So David owned his sin and cast himself on the loving, compassionate mercy of God for forgiveness. Of course he could not bring Uriah back form the dead, nor restore Joab's confidence in him. Nor could he stop the ongoing results of his sin, such as the death of the child he had had with Bathsheba (2 Sam. 12:14-18). What was done was done. But God could cleanse him and restore him and use him in measure again, and his soul began to thirst for this experience.

When David prayed, "cleanse me with hyssop," he was really asking God to "un-sin" him. Hyssop was a little fluffy plant used by the priests; they would dip it into the blood of the sacrifices and use it to sprinkle that blood over vessels and people to be cleansed ("un-sinned") in the temple. Lepers who had been healed would be sprinkled. And indeed, David wanted the hyssop of a leper's cleansing. Only God can make us feel "wholesome" when sin has done its leprous work in our lives. Don't you long for God to do that for you? To sense internally that the sin is undone, even though it has indeed been done, is an experience of cleansing that only God can work in our hearts.

Then David, experiencing the first relief of God's forgiveness, turned his thoughts toward his next step of renewal. Remember, he was running on empty. Now he realized that he had been coasting down the road of life on his past acts and godly reputation and had slammed hard against a gate—the gate of repentance. But gates can open onto gateways, and this one yielded to confession, making it possible for David to walk into a whole new life that God could create for him (Ps. 51:10).

When the Spirit of God forgives us, that is only the beginning! It's just the start of spiritual renewal. But let's be careful to understand what we are talking about here. Renewal is not a psychological catharsis that lasts a few hours or days. Renewal is a process. And David sang about this in his magnificent psalm.

When true repentance and renewal have taken place, there is a new sense of his presence (Ps. 51:11). God is "close," nearer than breathing. We are searingly aware that "he is." Then there is the "joy of our salvation" to contend with (51:12). Yes, to contend with! We find ourselves surprised by joy as we wake on a Monday morning and discover ourselves running hand in hand with happiness through dark valleys filled with wolves, bears, and lions! Joy overtakes our gray spirits, painting them with rainbow rays, refusing to let our lives be mediocre.

What is more, this experience will "last." David prayed for a willing spirit to "sustain" him. To keep him keeping on. He wanted that sustaining ability to enjoy the Lord and his work as he began to share again what God had done for him.

Oh yes! Repentance and renewal are far more than saying "sorry." They bear results: God will give you a willing spirit, an evangelist's heart, and a worldview!

"Then I will teach transgressors your ways, and sinners will turn back to you," said David (Ps. 51:13). Have you noticed how you don't care if people end up in heaven or in hell when there's unconfessed sin in your life? There will never be "fire in your bones" if the bones the Lord has crushed do not first rejoice in his personal dealings with you (51:8)!

And this worldview! What does it change? Well, it caused David to take a good look at Israel with new eyes. Zion and the people of God began to look different to him. There would be no more days in bed for him! The walls of Zion must be fortified, and the battles of the Lord must be fought. God's purposes were superimposed on his thinking again, diminishing the importance of his own personal plans and getting everything back into perspective.

Tell me, can you identify with David? Are you running on empty because of sin in your life that you think is well hidden? God sees and knows all about it. He wants you to face it, name it, confess it, turn from it, and, where you can, put things right. Self-flagellation will not make any lasting difference. Listen to David: "You do not delight in sacrifice, or I would bring it; you do not take pleasure in burnt offerings. The sacrifices of God are a broken spirit; a broken and contrite heart, O God, you will not despise" (Ps. 51:16-17).

God looks for brokenness of spirit—for a contrite, humble heart that, quickened by the Holy Spirit, teaches us to regard our sin as he does. We learn to pray, in the words of the old hymn:

> Throw light into the darkened cells,
> Where passion reigns within;
> Quicken my conscience till it feels
> The loathsomeness of sin.

And when we have seen our sin for what it is and rejected it, God will help us to have the right spirit in our hearts. Then we will be able to add:

Thus prostrate I shall learn of Thee,
What now I feebly prove,
That God alone in Christ can be
Unutterable love.

Refueling

1. Read 2 Samuel 11:1-12, 25.
   - (a) What could David and Bathsheba have done to avoid this situation?
   - (b) What can we do to avoid similar scenarios?
   - (c) Respond to this sentence: "If you walk deliberately into temptation, don't expect the Lord to deliver you from evil."
   - (d) Discuss friendship. How do we find friends like Jonathan and Nathan? How do we keep them?

2. Read Psalm 51.
   - (a) What do you discover from this psalm about:
       God?
       David?
       yourself?
   - (b) Which part of this psalm helps you, and why?

Prayer Time

If you have yielded to temptation, ask God to break your heart in the right sense. Let the experience finish its work in your life, and ask him to let your broken, contrite heart lead you to restoration and set you free to work again with power for your God.

4

Hannah

Broken Dreams

After [Samuel] was weaned, [Hannah] took the boy with her, young as he was, along with a three-year-old bull, an ephah of flour and a skin of wine, and brought him to the house of the Lord at Shiloh. When they had slaughtered the bull, they brought the boy to Eli, and she said to him, "As surely as you live, my lord, I am the woman who stood here beside you praying to the Lord. I prayed for this child, and the Lord has granted me what I asked of him. So now I give him to the Lord. For his whole life he will be given over to the Lord." And he worshiped the Lord there.

1 Samuel 1:24-28

*H*annah had been running on empty for some time. She had been aware of that, knew she was bound to come to a grinding halt soon, but had somehow kept going.

It was time to go to the temple at Shiloh for the feast, and that had kept her going for a while. Travel preparations had helped to keep her mind off herself. But once they all arrived at Shiloh, the distraction of the journey was over and there was nothing to *do* anymore. Then the empty feeling hung over Hannah like a menacing cloud.

Elkanah, her husband, had been working hard getting everyone settled. And Peninnah, his second wife, was busy with all her children. How Hannah would have loved to be busy with all her children. If she'd had any!

That was her problem, you see. Babies. Hopes never realized and dreams that had never come true. It had to do with the stigma that was attached to a woman who was infertile in her society. It was a horrible feeling deep down in the pit of her stomach. A want that kept on wanting. A chronic, draining emotional pain.

Elkanah returned from offering his sacrifice to the priest and began to give his family portions of the meat that was left over. The children crowded around their father, and he divided up the lesser parts among them. Then, having saved the best until last, he gave the choicest pieces to Hannah, his first love. Peninnah's eyes flashed. She was the one who had given Elkanah children. Her son was his firstborn! Why then did they not receive the best portions as the law dictated?

Poor Peninnah. When you've given your husband all you can possibly give him and it's never enough, what can you do but lash out at everyone in sight!

But Peninnah didn't lash out at everyone. She saved the brunt of her attack for Hannah, the "loved" wife. The focus of her anger was the one who was barren, and what more hurtful thing could she do than remind her constantly of that!

Do you find yourself anywhere in this story? Are you like Peninnah? Have you given your best and received little back from the people you love, till your bitterness has overflowed, emptying itself over the person who has the one thing you don't have but long to possess? Or are you like Hannah? Loved, yes, but longing for something to complete your life. Have you been looking to God to bring the gift of life to your deadness?

Both women in this situation were hurting bitterly. Peninnah was hurting because she had been used and felt like little more than a baby machine. Hannah was hurting because God had withheld her heart's desire—a child of her own. Hannah, however, did the right thing with her bitterness. She didn't let it spill all over her adversary, who "kept provoking her in order to irritate her" (1 Sam. 1:6). Hannah took her trouble to God.

There is nothing that will drain you more than bitterness! Bitterness eats you up inside, forcing you to eventually explode somewhere, sometime, at someone. It may be in a certain place, or because of a particular incident, or it may be a flash of memory that causes the explosion.

For Hannah it was the temple at Shiloh that did it. She had been here so many times before, and the smell of the burnt offerings, the familiar scenes in the courtyard, the figure of the old fat priest Eli leaning sleepily against the post must all have triggered memories too sharp to bear. How many times had she visited this place? How many prayers had been poured out in childlike hope? How many years of disappointment had intervened until there seemed to be no prayers left to pray? And then there was

Peninnah, viciously delighted to remind her month by month of her inadequacy.

When one of our own children had a difficult time conceiving, I suddenly found myself wanting to be a grandmother more than anything else in the world! I was glad of the feelings I began to experience on our children's behalf, because it helped me to understand a little of their deep struggle. Suddenly it seemed that everyone around us was getting pregnant and having babies—and I was buying shower gifts for others' celebrations! Everywhere we looked we saw babies. The magazines were full of them; the TV commercials featured them. Everyone was using cute little babies to sell their products. Even young mothers playing in the park with their children triggered that yearning feeling.

Maybe our struggle has been your struggle too. Or perhaps it is a longing to be married that has engendered bitterness. Or maybe you have had high hopes for a career opportunity or have had some special personal goal that has been thwarted. If this is the case, know that emptiness can invite bitterness to invade and control you. Suddenly, like Hannah, you can come to the end and find yourself running on empty. It's what we do at such times that determines our well-being and God's glory!

One of the things that exacerbates the problem is that people close to us don't seem to understand. Elkanah couldn't fully comprehend his beloved wife's anguish. Perhaps he was even unaware of Peninnah's hostility, most of which was caused, I am sure, by his unabashed favoritism. "Hannah, why are you weeping? Why don't you eat? Why are you downhearted? Don't I mean more to you than ten sons?" he asked his grieving wife (1 Sam. 1:8). Now the answer to that was obviously, "No, buddy, you don't!" But Hannah was not the sort of woman to give her husband such a bold answer. And he probably would not have understood, anyway. There are *some* things that only other women can fully understand, and in Hannah's case there was no other woman to care.

I remember being in the hospital, about to give birth to our first child. An efficient young nurse was assigned to me. She was neither married nor pregnant, and while her expertise in medical matters was quite apparent, somehow I couldn't help wishing the plump, motherly cleaning lady who was busy around my bed would put her mop down and tell me what it was like to bear a child. After all, she had had ten!

Empathy helps us a little, but both empathy and sympathy fall short in the long run. When you become obsessed with the notion that *only* the desired end can satisfy you, and the desired end is withheld, bitterness is bound to take over. That is, unless you turn it over to God. But how do you do that, you may ask, when God is the One who has the power to give you your heart's desire and has been busy withholding the very thing you beg him for? We can begin answering that question by paying attention to how Hannah dealt with it.

First of all, she talked it out—in prayer and in tears. That's where it has to begin. You need to get alone and start to tell God just how you feel about it all. Even if you've done that a thousand times before, you can do it one more time! Tell him about Peninnah, Elkanah, and the old priest who thinks you're drunk when you're praying because he's so out of touch with the Lord himself (1 Sam. 1:13). Tell him everything you've wanted to unload for, oh, so long!

It is not that God does not understand all of this, and it is certainly not that God has been detached or forgetful of your agony. It is not even that God is ignorant of the facts of the case. But it is necessary that you begin to tell him what is in your heart. Don't worry about what you sound like either; let the angry tears flow. And if you can't put the whole sad scene into words because you're so empty you even seem to be empty of words, just kneel down and say, "I am a prayer, Lord. Read me," and he will! You are, in fact, an open book to him. Read, marked, and learned, your story has already been recorded in heaven!

There is a beautiful therapy in this sort of praying, for the exercise of such heartfelt prayer eventually leads to hope! Unbelievably, after voicing her complaint, Hannah somehow found the power to ask for her heart's desire again. "O Lord Almighty," she prayed, "if you will only look upon your servant's misery and remember me, and not forget your servant but give her a son, then I will give him to the Lord for all the days of his life, and no razor will ever be used on his head" (1 Sam. 1:11).

This time, however, she had taken the final step toward resolution. It was a huge step for Hannah. She was *able to accept* whatever answer God was going to give her. Somehow, for the very first time, she was able to leave it with him! There was to be no more trying to twist God's arm with enough prayer to *make* him come through with the goods. No more hoping that enough shouting, crying, and tearing her hair out would touch the heart of God and extract a favor he had for some reason been withholding. Finally, yielding it all to God, she got up, wiped away her tears, and began to get on with her life.

I don't believe Hannah had ever let her frustration, agitation, or even her sense of isolation convince her that she was truly alone. Throughout her testing time she was convinced God was there—and therein lay her comfort. To accept that our prayers are heard and noted helps us to accept any answer when it comes, whether it be yes, no, or wait. A huge measure of peace lies in accepting God's answer—whatever it is.

The Bible says that Hannah's "face was no longer downcast" (1 Sam. 1:18). No more sadness, no more furrowed brow or taut lines around her mouth. She even ate a little and went on her way rejoicing (1 Sam. 1:18-19). Where did she go? Why, home, of course. Back to the same old house, the same old husband, the same old rival, and the same old situation. Ah, but she was not the same old Hannah! Somewhere back in Shiloh she had been able to give it all into God's hands and leave it there.

Have you ever had the experience of praying prayers like Hannah's but never knowing it to make any difference? I remember praying a fervent prayer when I was a young single woman of about twenty-one and wanted very much to be a young married woman of twenty-one. My fervent petition went something like this: "Please give me a husband, Lord. If you do, I will lend him to you as long as he lives. But if you don't, then that's okay. I'm willing to stay unmarried." Now I have to confess the last part of this prayer wasn't really true. I knew it should be said, and I determined it would be said, but I didn't say it very loud, and I was secretly hoping against hope that God either wouldn't hear that part of my prayer or would be so impressed with the high-sounding words he would give me a husband, even if he'd been planning not to!

Another time I remember praying ardently out loud at the end of a wonderful missionary challenge, "Lord, I am willing to go," while all the time I was secretly planning to stay. There will be no "peace that passes understanding" if we practice such parodies of prayer. There was certainly no joy in my heart until I was truly able to pray, "Lord, I really mean it—yes, I do! You can see my heart, so we both KNOW it's true!" Then, and only then, did the peace come.

Once Hannah had arrived at this point of abandonment of all her hopes and dreams, she was able to have a good cry, wash her face, get up and get on with it. She went home a new person to face the old problems.

We don't know how long it was after this that she got pregnant, but imagine the joy she and Elkanah experienced when her hopes were confirmed. God had indeed heard her prayers and given her a child! "I'll call him Samuel," she said, choosing the most suitable name, for Samuel means "God heard" (1 Sam. 1:20).

What joys and what tests now faced Hannah. Bigger than any she had met before. Hadn't she promised the Lord she would not keep the child, if there ever was a child? Can those of you who have borne children imagine giving them up? Surely Hannah must have been tempted to renege on her promises once Samuel was born. To keep the little one until he was three or even four and then give him up must have been sheer torture. Yet Hannah had promised God the child should serve him, and she kept her word. Taking little Samuel to the temple as soon as he was weaned, she left him there with Eli the priest.

After that, Hannah composed a song of praise and thanksgiving. Now I could imagine her writing a dirge or a sad ballad at this point—surely something in a minor key. But no, she wrote a song of joy so exquisite that Mary, the mother of our Lord, borrowed it to praise God (1 Sam. 2:1-10; Luke 1:46-55).

Hannah's song begins with the wonderful words: "My heart rejoices in the Lord." Now that is the whole thing; when the heart rejoices in the Lord and *not* in our circumstances, then the heart really rejoices! It laughs out loud. It sings and dances its way, day through dreary day, defying the gravity of tragedy or loss to pull it downward. When the source of our joy is God and not our husband, friends, or even our children—then we have discovered the secret of true happiness. God, who *is* joy, is ever with us. He never grows old, dies, goes on holiday, sues for divorce, or rejects us. Hannah left Samuel behind at Shiloh, but God opened the door to her when she got home!

But then God is the giver of joy and laughter, is he not? I always remember coming to Christ with a degree of trepidation, honestly believing that I would never laugh again. How the devil loves to tell us such lies. God created us for laughter; he made sure he gave us special face muscles to make it happen. I often think God himself must have laughed as he created this incredible universe. I'm sure he didn't make it with a frown on his face!

Hannah discovered God was not only the giver of laughter, but the giver of life as well. We *must* believe this too. Otherwise prayer would have no meaning at all. What is your prayer? Do you need life for a dying marriage, a dying child, a dying church, a dying faith? "The Lord brings death and makes alive," Hannah sang (1 Sam. 2:6). If we don't believe that God is the giver of life, then there is little hope that those we minister to will believe it either.

I have often told the tale of an adventure I had when I was alone in England. Because of the nature of our work, I had plenty of spare time on my hands. I lived in a sleepy little countryside, and my neighbors were rather elderly, living in delightful little rustic English cottages. The small churches in the area had few parishioners.

Could God bring life into such a dry situation, I wondered? Well, God, I believed, was the giver of life—so why not? At least we could ask him to work and see what his answer would be.

So we asked, and he gave some darling little old ladies—all in their seventies—for me to teach. I didn't know too much about little old ladies in their seventies, but it didn't take me long to realize it would take a miracle to change any of them! The older you get, the more set in your ways you become, or so it seems.

However, as I said, God had heard our prayers, and soon we were drowning in a sea of little old ladies. They came in all shapes and sizes, and true to 1 Samuel 2:6, we found that "The Lord brings death and makes alive." There were funerals to attend and "new births" to celebrate. God turned day into night and light into darkness, gave beauty for ashes and the oil of joy for mourning to these sweet mothers and grandmothers.

But God is not only the giver of life and laughter; he is also the giver of liberty. Hannah said, "He raises the poor from the dust and lifts the needy from the ash heap . . . for the Lord is a God who knows, and by him deeds are weighed" (1 Sam. 2:8, 3).

Now, remember, Hannah had just left Samuel in the hands of Eli—and in the hands of his sons Hophni and Phinehas! It was a well-known fact (these things *always* get talked about) that Eli's sons were "worthless fellows" and "wicked men" (1 Sam. 2:12 KJV, NIV). Many in Israel would have questioned Hannah's judgment. It seemed a crazy thing to do, to leave a young child with an old man and his wicked sons. Surely no mother in her right mind would willingly put her baby in such a place.

But God is the giver of liberty—liberty to do the right thing, no matter what people say! There is a joy in spiritual liberty, a wild abandonment that frees the spirit to sing. To be free from the bondage of "what will others think?" and "what will others say?" is liberty indeed!

Elkanah had said to Hannah, "Do what seems best to you," giving her freedom to stay at home and wean the child or freedom to take him to Shiloh when the time came (1 Sam. 1:21-24). So Hannah found the courage to keep her word to the Lord.

Have we exercised the liberty of doing the right thing—of keeping our vows to the Lord? In our marriage for instance. Have we kept our vow to be committed to our partner in sickness and in health, in poverty or wealth, for better of for worse, till death us do part? Or have we listened to people who say things like, "You owe it to yourself to get out of it"?

I know a young Christian girl who found the freedom to stick with a marriage that was sick, poor, and a whole lot worse than the best, healthy, wealthy bliss she had hoped for. Her family and friends urged her to end her marriage, and she had good biblical grounds for divorce. But she waited on the Lord and said, "I promised not only Jack, but the Lord, that I would stick with it. I'll keep my promise." Her marriage will probably never be what she hoped for, but now this middle-aged woman is a radiant, free person with a clear conscience and an infectious faith that over time is beginning to make an impact on her family for the Lord.

"What a waste," I overheard one woman say to another, on hearing that a brilliant young doctor had resigned his job to go to the mission field. "He said he promised God if he got through medical school, he would offer himself for full-time Christian service," she said with obvious disapproval. "Surely God would understand if he stayed here." The other woman agreed. "Look at his poor wife and child—what about them?"

Of course it's *always* harder to do the right thing when someone near and dear is going to feel the hurt. Samuel was Elkanah's son too, remember. His only son of his favorite wife. And what about Samuel himself? When Hannah took him to Shiloh, he was very young, perhaps only three years old (1 Sam. 1:24). Can you imagine what it must have been like for Samuel to be left behind by his mother? And then Hannah had to return home without him and face Peninnah's triumphant jibes. Now she was childless again, and I'm sure her "rival" used that to good effect.

But God is the One who takes pity on the poor and raises them up—who looks lovingly at the beggar and lifts him high. I'm sure Hannah felt both poor—bereft of her richest treasure—and beggarly indeed, able only to cast herself on the Lord for help. And he was there for her. "The Lord is a God who knows, and *by him deeds are weighed*" (1 Sam. 2:3). In the end, he is the One we have to give account to; he is the One who has heard our vows in the quiet of our bedroom or the shadow of the church pew, and has recorded our promises. He is the One who waits for us to give him Samuel! After all, we said we would.

What have you promised him? To read your Bible every day and spend time with him in prayer? Did you promise him money? Was there a mission project you promised to support? Did you promise God time? Time to serve in Sunday school? Time to be a youth sponsor? Time to serve on the church board? Did you promised him your soul, your life, your all? Did you promise him your "Samuel"? If so, have you kept your promise?

Oh, no one is saying you can present your Samuel to God without sacrifice. Hannah went to Shiloh with her baby boy *and* her sacrifice (1 Sam. 1:24-25). Yet sacrifice speaks of liberty too. We are free to bring the gift and the sacrifice, and we are free to stay at home and bring nothing. But once we have promised God the gift and the sacrifice, we are no longer free to withhold what we have promised.

Others may judge us whether we stay at home or whether we go to Shiloh (they will probably judge us for doing either), but God is the only true Judge. He is the One by whom all our actions are tried. He knows if our promises are kept. It must have been awfully tempting to promise the sacrifice and the child and then only bring the sacrifice! No one would have known if Hannah had done that. Except God! But God knew, and he was waiting at Shiloh for Samuel.

And God knew what it meant to give an only son. Hannah did not need to fear what he would do with her Samuel or with her. Just look at what happened.

Oh, God didn't get rid of Peninnah for her, but he did bless Hannah in a very special way. He blessed her with more children. God said "Thank you" to Hannah in his own way (1 Sam. 2:18-21). Though Hannah's story is not a "happily ever after" one, I believe Hannah was happy ever after. Because God is indeed the giver of life, the giver of laughter, and the giver of liberty!

Do you struggle with a hard choice as you read these words? Is there a right action you are absolutely sure God wants you to take? Do you hesitate because those around you try to persuade you otherwise? Remember, they don't know the vows that have been made between you and God. Let me encourage you to do the right thing—even if humanly speaking you might be monetarily poorer because of it, or criticized for going too far.

Please hear what I am saying. This is *not* an invitation to irresponsibility! Hannah was not being irresponsible. She was following through on her vow to the Lord.

Did you make a vow to the Lord to keep your children under the sound of God's Word? Did you promise him to have them in church? Have there been many "good," sensible reasons to renege on that promise? Was the church too cold; were the people hypocrites; was Eli not the best teacher around? Did you think if you were a good Hannah your Samuels would be better off with you at home? Did they cling to your hand when you tried to leave them? Were they too young and immature to understand that while what you were doing might not have been the easiest thing for them or for you, while it might not have made them particularly happy at the time, it was where they needed to be? Did you keep your promise to God?

For a long time I led a junior high youth group. This was the most frustrating group on earth to work with, and it was also the most rewarding. The parents would battle to get their kids there, and too often they would give up.

"The kids don't like it," they would tell me.

"Neither did Samuel," I would reply.

"They won't learn anything if they don't like it," they would reason. "And they don't have any friends in the group."

"Neither did Samuel," I would answer.

"But they don't understand the talks—they're too grown-up for them, and anyway," they would say triumphantly, "we've heard two of your leaders' lives are not quite what they should be!"

"Well," I would say in quick defense of my colleagues, "they are miles ahead of Hophni and Phinehas!"

"We want our children at home that night so we can have a family time," they would explain, knowing I couldn't object to that. "They're out every other night at school activities, you see," they would reason.

I would then suggest that they cut out some school activities for the sake of their family time and that they keep their vows to the Lord. In the end, that was the only thing that would encourage them to tell their junior high kids they *were* going to come whether they wanted to or not. That cooperation then enabled me to be able to win those kids to myself, and then to the Lord. After all, the vows those parents made were to God—not to the children nor the Sunday school nor the church, but to him.

And Samuel did just fine. He grew up under Eli's tutelage, came to know the Lord, and went on to become one of Israel's most famous and godly leaders.

Hannah went home from the temple rejoicing, singing her beautiful song. For relinquishment leads to rejoicing, and obedience leads to freedom. And sacrifice leads to fullness of life and blessing for those you love best.

As someone has most aptly said, "If thou wouldst raise a Samuel, be thyself a Hannah." This way, neither you nor your child will be found running on empty.

Refueling

1. Read 1 Samuel 1.
   - (a) What can you learn from Hannah's prayer?
   - (b) Think about why and how Hannah relinquished her son. Can you identify? How?

2. Read 1 Samuel 2.
   - (a) How well did Hannah know God? Make a list of the things she knew about the Lord's character.
   - (b) Which particular characteristics do you think helped her at such a time of stress?
   - (c) Think about this phrase: "God is the giver of life—laughter—liberty." Which point especially strikes you, and why? Which aspect of the chapter is the greatest challenge to you?

Prayer Time

Pray that, like Hannah, you will keep the vows you have made to the Lord. Pray for your Samuels.

5

Jonah

Disobedience

From inside the fish Jonah prayed to the Lord his God. He said:

"In my distress I called to the Lord,
and he answered me.
From the depths of the grave I called for help,
and you listened to my cry.
You hurled me into the deep,
into the very heart of the seas,
and the currents swirled about me;
all your waves and breakers
swept over me.
I said, 'I have been banished
from your sight;
yet I will look again
toward your holy temple.'"

Jonah 2:1-4

*B*ecause Jonah was running on empty, a certain fish was running on full! It required a miracle for Jonah to be swallowed by such a fish (or, as some would have it, a whale): the obliging animal needed to be right under the boat that carried Jonah at exactly the moment he was thrown overboard. And all of this in the middle of a storm with the vessel pitching and tossing every which way. Of course, God was equal to the challenge, orchestrating it all as Jonah plunged to the depths, beginning his great adventure.

It's hard to know just where Jonah's nightmare really started. Perhaps it began with his disobedience; the prophet was running away from God. He was foolish enough to think he could escape the Lord's presence. In fact, he was about to find out for himself the truth of David's words, "Where can I go from your Spirit? Where can I flee from your presence? If I go up to the heavens, you are there; if I make my bed in the depths, you are there. If I rise on the wings of the dawn, if I settle on the far side of the sea, even there your hand will guide me, your right hand will hold me fast" (Ps. 139:7-10).

Jonah was trying to run away from something he didn't want to do. God had told him to go to the city of Nineveh, and instead of obeying, he had boarded a ship bound for Tarshish—which was exactly in the opposite direction. Even though Jonah was God's man of the moment, this was the moment he chose not to be the man God called him to be.

It's easy to criticize Jonah, for he represents the whole heart of humanity that is at war with God. We humans don't like God's presence or his programs. We want to go our own way and plan our own lives. Yet somehow we imagine that God's men and women always love him easily and delight in the things he asks them to do. We imagine Mrs. Noah loved animals, for instance. After all, God surely would not have expected her to be cooped up in the ark with them all that time if she didn't. But what if Mrs. Noah hated furry creatures—or had allergies—or got seasick? What if old Noah himself slipped a disk while he was building the big boat, or got bitten by a snake, or didn't get along with one of his daughters-in-law? We cannot just *assume* it was all so easy for them.

The will of God is not always easy. Sometimes it is kittens and robins, koala bears and woolly lambs. But at other times it's snakes and reptiles, lions and tigers, and whales! And what if Jonah couldn't swim? What if he feared fish—especially big fish?

It was not too hard for me to pack up our family and immigrate to another country. But it was very hard for me, once the immigration was done, to accept the ministry God gave to me. Somehow the ark looks very different when you are building it, than it does from the kitchen window when you're actually living inside.

I don't know just how and where Jonah had met the Lord and committed himself to being God's man, but I do know, because the Scripture tells us, that there came a day he decided he'd had enough of the job he had been given to do. It was not turning out one bit like he thought it would! By the time we meet Jonah, we see only his disobedience and the storm it caused in the heavens above and in the depths below. But fierce though this storm was, Jonah was oblivious to it. He was asleep (Jon. 1:5).

How he could have slept through such cataclysm is beyond me, but sometimes we can so chloroform our conscience that nothing seems to wake us to reality. Jonah knew very well he was running away from the Lord; he had even told the sailors on the ship that this was the case (Jon. 1:10). But a certain psychological effect can put us "out of it." There is a slumbering peace that takes over when we give up trying to do the right thing.

If a man and woman are struggling to keep their marriage intact, for example, there can be a lot of turmoil involved. To separate from each other, and thereby remove themselves from the battle zone, results in a peace that's very easy to understand. It's called the peace of giving up! I have had women tell me that they have a certain "peace" since they have walked away from their responsibilities to their husband and children to follow their heart's attraction for another man. That peace is *not* the peace of God! Those ladies may well sleep through the storm for a little while, but someone or something will all too soon shake them awake to the awful reality that surrounds them.

Jonah, shaken awake by the sailors' rough hands, realized he could not run away any longer. His disobedience had begun to affect everyone else around him. That's what disobedience does, of course. Your storm becomes theirs! The world begins to fall apart, and innocent people get hurt. It's amazing how one person's disobedience causes a storm for every single person in sight!

A couple may honestly believe that it is "best" for the children if they split up. That way the kids won't have to live in an atmosphere of conflict, they reason. But they don't realize the storm that is brewing ahead as the siblings are separated and have to battle with the sudden and unexpected new mom or dad who is no relation to them whatsoever and is "taking the place" of their own mom or dad. Add the complication of strange new grandparents and the absence of loved familiar ones, and it seems a whole vessel full of people are sharing your own personal storm. It's a brave parent who can say at this point: "Some of this is my fault! I own my part of the fault and failure, and I must bear the consequences for my own part of the action, and cast myself on the mercy of the Lord!"

Jonah was one such brave man. There was absolutely no doubt in his mind who was to blame for the storm. He told the sailors he was responsible and, concerned for their safety, told them to throw him overboard (Jon. 1:12). Now I'm obviously not advocating that you throw yourself into the river if you've made a mess of your life! God doesn't have a whale waiting for you in the Potomac or Mississippi! What I *am* saying is this: Face reality, own up to your part of the fault and failure, and cast yourself on God's mercy. He will be waiting for you.

The amazing thing about trying to run away from God is the stupidity of it. After all, he has longer legs than we have! And what energy! He has never run on empty in all his years of eternity! Since Adam and Eve first ran behind the tree of sin, many of their sons and daughters have done the same—run away from God. Jacob ran from the rightful wrath of Esau, having stolen his blessing and his birthright. David ran from his responsibilities straight into Bathsheba's arms. And Jonah ran from Nineveh. Men and women have always known how to run away from the Lord. What they haven't understood so often is how futile it is!

I suppose most of us have had a "Nineveh" experience in our lives. For some it was a responsibility God gave to us, or a vocation he called us to follow. For others, it was a challenge to grapple with, or a relationship that needed to be mended. For still others, it was a serious illness. When God tells us to go and do something about our Nineveh, we can confront the challenge or run away from it. And it saves us and God an awful lot of trouble if we do what we are told!

Nineveh has been many things to me. At one point in my life, Nineveh was working with young people. I knew God had told me to do something about the wild young folk who roamed the streets of my hometown, but it took me a little while to obey. Another time my Nineveh was working with women. After immigrating to America, God told me to take on this ministry. This time I really ran to Tarshish! I got as far away as I could from any involvement in women's ministries! But God engineered a set of circumstances that locked me in until I began to obey him. As surely as Jonah could not escape from the fish carrying him to Nineveh, I could not escape from being in the constant company of women.

In the same way Jonah could not escape God's command: "And the Lord commanded the fish, and it vomited Jonah onto dry land" (Jon. 2:10). And then "the word of the Lord came to Jonah a second time" (Jon. 3:1). After the wind and the whale came the Word! The wind and the storm cause us to wake up to the reality of things, while the whale gives us a chance to put things right with God. God's second chances do not always come to those who run away from the first chances, but they often do, and God's mercy is a wonderful grace. He doesn't always give us all we deserve.

The message God had for Jonah hadn't changed, but the man who received it had! Who knows just why Jonah set off at a brisk trot as soon as he got his second opportunity, but we can guess. Perhaps he thought the fish would follow him right up onto the dry ground and swallow him again if he didn't get going. Or he may have feared an even worse fate would await him if he dragged his heels. Whatever his motive, some obedience was better than no obedience! So "Jonah obeyed the word of the Lord and went to Nineveh" (Jon. 3:3).

Jonah was beginning to get the message, and it was a disturbing one for him: God loved the Ninevites! Now why did this bother him so? Because Jonah didn't love the Ninevites. In fact, he hated them! They were Israel's enemies. He wanted God to kill them, not bless them. He knew that other prophets had predicted that God would use the Ninevites to punish Israel for her apostasy. Jonah, being a true blue Jew, and having tunnel vision, was not interested in the big picture. The fact that God had set Israel aside to be his missionary nation, that all the nations of the world might eventually be blessed through her, was of little consequence to Jonah. The only thing he was thinking about was the here and now and Israel's safety. If he preached to Nineveh and Nineveh repented, God would not judge her and wipe her out; and if God did not judge her and wipe her out, she would be strong enough to hurt Israel. Jonah wanted no part of that. At that moment he loved his country far more than he loved his God!

Now came the dilemma. Jonah had had an incredible experience inside the fish's stomach. To be swallowed by a fish and find yourself still alive is not anyone's idea of something to do on a Sunday afternoon! But he *had* survived, and in the midst of his terrible ordeal God had heard his prayer and visited him (Jon. 2). Now he dared not disobey again, so he grudgingly set out to do the will of God!

But Jonah had yet a larger lesson to learn. God loves all humanity, including Ninevites and Jonahs. He was just as concerned for his stubborn, unhappy, battered, and bruised prophet as he was for the unhappy, cruel, heathen Assyrians. So even as the petulant Jonah plodded down the road, God was at work on his behalf. God would meet him by the side of the road in the heat of the day. He would provide for Jonah. He would care for him. He would speak lovingly with him. He would bless him. He would, in effect, fill up his empty spirit so that Jonah could quit running on empty!

Jonah must have been well aware that his spirit was empty. Even though he had been able to pray, he was still angry about a lot of things, and chronic anger empties your spirit as soon as God fills it up! Anger burns a hole in your heart so that all the blessings leak out!

In his trouble, though, Jonah had been able to remember the Word of God. Chapter 2 is full of Scripture quotes he used in his desperate prayer to the Lord. But the head can be full of Scripture and the heart empty of its blessings! And so it was with Jonah. His ministry had been powerful, and lives had been changed as he preached to the Ninevites (Jon. 3), yet he seemed to be powerless to change his own attitude!

But the Word of God is the Word of God, and it will do the things that need doing to the people who respond to it—even if the preacher is out of sorts. As Jonah preach his way through Nineveh, people listened, repented, and re-sponded in such a dimension that Jonah had a full-scale revival on his hands. It's amazing what you can do right when what you feel is all wrong!

Years ago I was angry with God for taking my husband away from the family for long terms of ministry. I was very much like Jonah. I was afraid to rebel openly for fear God might send a whale after me. I was sure something awful might happen if I didn't go through the motions of being a good little missionary wife. I knew it was right to teach my Bible classes because right is right, and truth is truth, even though my heart was bitter and I was empty of joy.

I knew that the Word of God was still the Word of God. Didn't the Bible say that it is a lamp and a light, a hammer and a sword that will accomplish God's work in people's lives? Well, I saw the Word of God do the good work it promised, and people did come to Christ. Ninevites' lives were changed and filled, while I, the messenger of these good tidings, was empty and miserable, and still as angry as ever. I discovered, however, even as Jonah had discovered thousands of years before me, that God was just as concerned for me as he was for the Ninevites!

God loved me and knew that anger robbed me of all the inner joy and delight he longed for me to experience. I also came to realize that he was concerned that I was missing the joy of loving the Ninevites as he loved them! Only people who love the Ninevites know the heavenly joy when one of them comes to the Lord. Jonah didn't love the Ninevites, and he was "greatly displeased and became angry" when they repented (Jon. 4:1). Things were just as bad as he had feared they would be when the Word of the Lord first came to him and told him to go and preach to Nineveh. Jonah was truly running on empty; he had reached the bottom of the tank.

Perhaps you are finding this a little difficult to understand. Why was Jonah so upset? Surely even a prejudiced man can find it in his heart to be glad over one sinner who repents—never mind a whole city of them from king to commoner! Well, consider this. Suppose a man robbed and raped your elderly mother, tortured your ailing father, and ran off with your daughter, holding her in terror while he demanded ransom. Then, after this monster of a man was caught and tried, the judge told him that if he was truly sorry and promised not to do it again, he would set him free. How would you feel? Yes, that's how Jonah felt, too! But what would you have thought had the judge then gone on to explain that this same man had actually done all this, and more, to the judge's family too?

You see, any sin against a person is a sin against God. So God counts any and all sins, against any and all people, as sins actually done not only to his family, but to him. And when the sinner, whoever he or she is, repents, it is God who forgives!

Jonah got a vivid lesson from God, for he learned that God cares for people who don't care about anything or anyone. He learned that God's love is as broad as the skies, as deep as the night, and as strong as a nuclear explosion. God showed Jonah that he made everything and cares about everything that he made. He showed it through the story of the vine that mysteriously shot up overnight and shaded the prophet from the hot sun (Jon. 4:6). When the vine withered, when the hot sun and searing wind came, Jonah began to understand how awful it was to have no shelter from the terrible heat! But he was only beginning to learn the lesson of how much more terrible it was to have no shade for one's sinful soul against the hot wrath of God.

"Have you any right to be angry?" God asked Jonah, implying most definitely that he did not (Jon. 4:4). Anger is the root from which murder springs. And this un-abated, uncontrolled anger led the Ninevites to treat their slaves in the cruelest ways. Yet Jonah, who prided him-self on never being able to treat another human being in such a fashion, was guilty of worse—of wanting them to go to hell!

"Should I not be concerned about that great city?" God asked Jonah (Jon. 4:11). Those people are ignorant. They have never had a chance to be different. Give them a chance and see what they will do. Why, God says, "Nineveh has more than a hundred and twenty thousand people who cannot tell their right hand from their left" (4:11). What sort of people do not know which hand is right and which is left? Why, children, of course. Nineveh was a city full of children! "And many cattle as well," the Lord added (4:11). What a touch from our Creator; the One who fashioned the gentle dove and gave the leopard its spots rejoiced to provide another "ark" of deliverance for his creation.

I believe Jonah finally got the message. Why? Because he wrote the book! It is his testimony to the fact that God is love, and that he loves his sinful and stubborn prophets who are running on empty as much as he loves Ninevites bound for eternal damnation.

We must catch Jonah's heartbeat—his mission heart. To do that, we will first of all need to obey. Like Jonah, we will probably have to do that without any nice, warm, fuzzy feelings at the start. Whatever Jonah was experiencing as he marched through Nineveh preaching his heart out, it was not a fit of the warm fuzzies!

Or, if we can't identify with Jonah, perhaps we can identify with the little worm God sent to eat the vine (Jon. 4:7). He certainly found that obedience doesn't always taste sweet! Just think of that poor little worm. The job God chose for him was no little piece of cake—nor a little piece of vine to be more precise! Worms don't usually eat six-foot vines! But the Word says, "God provided a worm." He specially prepared the little thing, for God never calls without equipping. Even a worm can do what God wants him to do if he'll obey his Maker. Perhaps we cannot identify with Jonah—after all, we don't think of ourselves as mighty prophets—but what about identifying with the little worm?

Have you ever looked at Nineveh as Jonah looked at it—or at the vine as the little worm did—and wanted to turn tail and run? What right thing has God called you to do? What words must be written, what phone call made, what relationship mended, what peace restored? What teenager needs confronting, or what elderly person needs to be cared for? What action has God's voice been directing you to take? Will you obey?

Do you even know how to start? For if you do not start, it is certain you will never finish! Why not take a lesson from the little worm? Just take the first bite. Do the first obvious thing. Even if you think it will poison you, do it anyway. Don't worry about the second bite, or the third, or the fourth. Just start, and soon you will have finished the whole thing.

Sometimes it is the size of the problem that puts us off. I remember a friend of mine being absolutely devastated because her daughter had written from college telling her she was sleeping with her boyfriend. Now she wanted to bring the boy home to meet her parents.

This was a Nineveh for my friend, but she didn't feel she was a Jonah. "Perhaps you can better identify with the little worm," I suggested. That she could do. I encouraged her to take the first bite, to do *one* obvious thing. "Pick up a pen and write a reply to your daughter, assuring her of God's love and yours, but stating your disapproval on scriptural grounds about her lifestyle," I suggested. She was able to do this. And then it was somehow possible to do the next thing she had truly thought was impossible. To invite them both to come home. One thing led to the next, and after many months the young man was reached for Christ, and eventually her daughter was restored to the Lord.

Start with one bite—the one thing you can do. The things you can't do will wait for another day. One obedience lends strength and builds you up for the next.

I like to think Jonah came down from his holy hill of disdain and went back into Nineveh and became their prophet. Why not? Strange things happen when you're running on full! When God meets you in the depths, as he did Jonah, and sends you off to do his will, he changes you as you go, and gives you needed fuel.

In the course of my work I met a young man one day who was greatly in need. He was a wild teenager—a

Ninevite, if you like. I won his confidence, and he took me to meet his friends. They were Ninevites, too. They roamed the city streets, looking for trouble and finding it. I knew God wanted me to explain the gospel to them, but I didn't want to. I much preferred the "Israelites"—the churched kids I taught in Sunday school. For a while I ran away from this challenge, but God sent a whale of a circumstance into my life to make me face my particular Nineveh: this wild young man got into trouble and was arrested. He gave my name as his friend, and I ended up at the police station. They even sent a black "fish" (a police car) to get me! Shaken by this event, I decided I'd better get involved.

I didn't have a clue where to start. But like a little worm, I took the first bite—I did the obvious thing. I simply got on a bus and went to where the Ninevites lived—downtown. I found them, talked to them, and eventually found myself loving them as God did. I caught Ninevitis! I discovered, as Jonah did, that the Ninevites hadn't rejected Christ; they just hadn't had a chance to receive him! As God worked with me, and with them, I stayed in their town and became their "prophet." And one day I realized I was running on full! Full of joy and excitement, full of purpose and plans, full of peace—full of God!

Disobedience empties your life, but obedience fills it to overflowing.

Refueling

---

1. Read Jonah 1. What do you learn about:
   - (a) Jonah?
   - (b) the sailors?
   - (c) the Lord?

---

2. Read Jonah 2. What five things do you learn about prayer from this chapter?

---

3. Read Jonah 3. What do you learn about:
   - (a) preaching?
   - (b) preachers?

---

4. Read Jonah 4. What do you learn about yourself?

Prayer Time

Pray for people like the Ninevites who need people like Jonah to minister to them. And pray for people like Jonah to go.

6

The Prodigal Sons

Rebellion

"Meanwhile, the older son was in the field. When he came near the house, he heard music and dancing. So he called one of the servants and asked him what was going on. 'Your brother has come,' he replied, 'and your father has killed the fattened calf because he has him back safe and sound.'

"The older brother became angry and refused to go in. So his father went out and pleaded with him. But he answered his father, 'Look! All these years I've been slaving for you and never disobeyed your orders. Yet you never gave me even a young goat so I could celebrate with my friends. But when this son of yours who has squandered your property with prostitutes comes home, you kill the fattened calf for him!'

" 'My son,' the father said, 'you are always with me, and everything I have is yours. But we had to celebrate and be glad, because this brother of yours was dead and is alive again; he was lost and is found.' "

Luke 15:25-32

Once upon a time there was a wealthy landowner who had two sons. He loved them both dearly and lavished good things upon them. He provided them with a big house, a lovely garden, and rewarding work to do. But all this wasn't enough for the younger son. He wanted his freedom. He wanted to see the world. And so his father gave him all his inheritance and told him he was free to go.

This is the beginning of one of the most famous parables Jesus told. All of Jesus' stories reflected his great concern for those who were running on empty! When Jesus told this particular parable, he hoped his listeners would see themselves individually in the character of the elder brother, see humanity as a whole in the younger son, and see God the Father in the wealthy landowner. And so he continued his story. . . .

At first, everything was wonderful. The younger son traveled to a far country, where he spent his resources freely on himself and his new friends. But he was cut off from his father now, and once his funds were gone, they were gone. Then his situation became desperate. His fair-weather friends forsook him, and he ended up hiring himself out to feed pigs just to get a few scraps to eat. Now, for a good little Jewish boy to end up in a pigsty meant he had gone about as far away from his father as he could go. (Jews have as little to do with pigs as possible!) He was a long way from his roots. He was truly "running on empty."

There is no indication that the listeners to Jesus' story—the Pharisees—responded. They were not noted for caring much about prodigal people who ended up in pigsties—especially pigsties of their own making (Luke 15:1-2). But if the Pharisees of Jesus' day could not identify, I can!

I see myself "in a glass clearly." Raised in a wonderful family and given everything I could possibly want, I took it all, headed for the far country, and wasted my life with rebellious living. I was far from God and ended up in a pigsty—hungry, dirty, and empty!

Now, there are all sorts of pigsties. There are pretty pigsties, posh pigsties, piggy pigsties, and priggy pigsties. Mine was full of prigs. Nice, educated people who didn't even know they were in a pigsty—just like me.

Then one day I came to my senses. It's amazing how that happens. Parents who are worried about their children who are not embracing their faith can take courage; after all, the young prodigal came to his senses in the pigsty—not in the pew! God is surely just where they are, for he is everywhere in his world. God the Father has a missionary heart!

I happened to be in the hospital at the time. I had cause to think, and realized I was living a life far from the lifestyle I had been brought up to live. It was hard for me to admit I was a sinner and needed to ask my Father for forgiveness, but when you realize you're spiritually dirty, hungry, and empty—when even the pigs around you look clean, fat, and satisfied by comparison—that helps!

"I will set out and go back to my father and say to him: Father, I have sinned against heaven and against you. I am no longer worthy to be called your son; make me like one of your hired men," the young man in the story said with sudden resolve as he saw his own sin (Luke 15:18-19).

Sin is an odd thing. When *you* begin playing with it, you find it hard to believe *it* will end up playing with you! But sin does that, of course. Like the circus owner who bought a baby snake and began to play with it. The snake was so small that he could easily have ground it to death with the heel of his shoe. As the snake grew, the man trained it to wrap itself round his body—a wonderful act of courage.

Then one day, when it was fully grown, the snake crushed the man to death. Sin will do that if you insist on playing with it long enough.

But like the young man in the story, we *do* have a choice. We don't have to continue playing with sin; we don't have to sit in the pigsty; we can do something about our empty condition. We can go home to the Father.

I well remember the night I said to myself, "I'M GOING HOME!" I didn't know what I was going to say to my Father, but my friend, who was one of my Father's servants, helped me. Falteringly, I prayed a prayer that went something like this: "I've sinned against heaven and against a whole lot of other people, Father, and I'm so very sorry. Through a set of circumstances outside my control, and some I brought on myself, I'm sitting in a pigsty—a place I now believe you didn't have in mind when you created me. Make me one of your servants, Lord." I didn't feel worthy even to talk to my Father in heaven, and for the first time in my life I knew I really wasn't fit to be in his presence, but I came home anyway. I was so sure he would be there waiting for me. What I didn't know was how happy he would be to see me!

When Jesus told this parable of the lost son, he told of a father watching for his prodigal to return. You get the feeling that the man watched the road every day, waiting to catch a glimpse of his boy coming home. Jesus said that this is exactly what happens in heaven. The Father and his angels are watching a whole world full of prodigals sitting in packed-out pigsties! And whenever one comes to their senses and starts out for home, the Father leans out of heaven, alerting the angels, and says, "Look, there's one!" (Luke 15:7).

When I was fourteen years old and hadn't a serious thought in my empty little head, I remember looking at a Bible on a bookshelf and struggling with myself.

"Read it," insisted a little voice inside.

"What for?" I argued, "I don't need it."

"You don't even know what's inside," said the voice, "so how can you know you don't need it! Go on, take it down off the shelf and open it up."

"No," I answered stubbornly.

The funny thing was that I suddenly wanted to but something held me back. I never did obey that still, small voice, but I do believe at that initial moment of spiritual awakening in my young heart, the Father turned to the angels, pointed me out, and said, "She's coming home!" I didn't arrive until five years later, when I realized that the Father of love runs down the road of repentance and meets us at the cross. He does not make us crawl home, because his Son already crawled to Calvary for us, carrying our cross on his back! It's such a powerful picture, it leaves me breathless.

God's grace is an amazing thing. God's truth tells us the truth about ourselves, but his grace forgives us for the truth he reveals!

> "You reap what you sow—you know,"
> said Truth.
>
> Grace agreed, then set off—
> running hard—
> toward the tired boy stumbling home.
> Truth kept pace, declaring
> in a loud voice
> what had been done.
> The boy waited awkwardly—
> acknowledging Truth's presence,
> wondering who Grace was.
>
> "You reap what you sow—you know,"
> said Truth—with truth.

The boy nodded, eyes on his bare feet,
   clutching his rags around him,
      ashamed of the dirt!
Grace told Truth to stop nagging—
   "After all," he said,
   "Nagging is unforgiveness
      showing—and that's not
         your job."
      Grace addressed the boy:
         "I forgive you," he said.

"He doesn't deserve it,"
            said Truth—with truth!

Grace agreed,
   and then forgave him,
      anyway,
   because that's what Grace does
      all the time!
Grace bent low and helped the boy
      onto his feet—
   the boy felt holes in the Man's
      hands.
He was close enough now
   to see Grace had
      a broken
         heart
   and crucified feet.
      It must have hurt him dreadfully
         to run down the road
            like that.

The boy cried then
   as he had never cried before—
      great tears of terrible sorrow,

for suddenly he recognized
the Stranger . . .

. . . He had his Father's eyes!

In the story of the prodigal son, Jesus used three beautiful symbols to show how thoroughly the Father welcomes us home.

The first is the robe that the father offered to cover the son's rags—the robe of righteousness covering our unrighteousness. We cannot manufacture our own garment of grace to hide the dirt and the mess our lives are in. God needs to do that for us. The Bible promises us that God covers our past as surely as the father in this wonderful story covered the prodigal's rags.

Secondly, the father put shoes on his son's feet. Only slaves went barefoot; sons wore shoes! Footwear enabled the wearer to walk as a prince among men. As such, shoes symbolize the provision that the Father gives all prodigals who return in repentance and contrition to him. This footwear helps us "walk through life" properly—as princes, not prodigals.

And finally, the father put a ring on his son's hand. This ring had an image of the father's face on it and was used as a stamp or seal to do the father's business in the world. "Is the stamp of my Father's image on the work that I do, or is there only the stamp of my own likeness?" is the question I often ask myself, as well as, "And what is that work?" Well, it involves catching the Father's vision and getting involved in those projects close to his heart. And this brings us to the story of the older brother.

When you look at the elder brother in the story, you get the feeling that he didn't know his father's heart very well. You also get the decided impression that he didn't care whether his brother ever came home or not.

The elder brother complained that he had been treated like a slave, rather than a son. "All these years I've been slaving for you," he said (Luke 15:29). Now this is an amazing statement in light of verse 31, and in view of the beginning of the story. When the younger son asked for his inheritance, the older brother was looking right over his shoulder, and the father "divided his property between them" (Luke 15:12). All this time the son had in fact been working for himself! As his father reminded him, "everything I have is yours" (15:31).

If we have no sense of "ownership" in our work for the Lord, then there is a good possibility we will indeed feel like slaves instead of sons. Slaves were unrewarded and unappreciated; they had no rights and they had nothing to call their own. But the Bible tells us we are "heirs of God and co-heirs with Christ" (Rom. 8:17). When we understand that all that we are is his and all that he is, is ours, we will see that God is not expecting unreasonable things from us.

I have met my share of "older brothers" in the church. They expect public appreciation for everything they do and demand remuneration for their "spiritual" service. And they shun the hard, "dirty" work they feel is beneath their dignity.

"I have *never* disobeyed your orders," the elder brother boasted self-righteously, yet he had just refused to go in to his father's party. He didn't understand that his father was not looking for tight-lipped, bitter obedience. He wanted his son to have a rejoicing spirit. "This brother of yours was dead and is alive again; he was lost and is found" he said. "We *had* to celebrate" (Luke 15:32). But the older brother refused to rejoice over the sinner who had repented. To refuse to go in to the father's party was a funny sort of obedience, don't you think?

The older brother was not only a self-righteous creature, but also a self-centered one. He wanted a party all for himself and his friends, not in someone else's honor (Luke

15:29). Sadly, as a result, all the years of his labor counted for nothing.

Of course, all this leads inevitably to the older brother's attitude toward his younger brother. Apparently the older brother had never thought it necessary to put his father's mind at ease and go searching for his younger brother in the far country. He had never caught his father's vision nor felt his father's heartbeat. But then, an older brother who stays near the mansion all his life and never ventures onto the mission field counts his responsibility toward his younger brother very lightly. "This son of yours," he complained to the father, whereupon the father quietly reminded him, "This brother of yours." You can almost hear the older brother saying bitterly, "Am I my brother's keeper?" And hear the father's quick reply, "No, but you are your brother's brother!"

If we are out of touch with the lost, we are not suddenly going to find our hearts overflowing with compassion when they come home! And I don't believe our hearts will ever be touched unless we get ourselves involved in the mission!

The older brother fraternizes only with those who are just like him! Like finds like. Pharisees deal only with Pharisees, and they don't feel comfortable outside their own circle. But it was the fattened calf that proved to be the last straw.

The older brother wanted the younger to *pay*, not play! He wanted him to get what he deserved. This vindictive spirit led him to burst out with his long-buried resentments. "But when this son of yours who has squandered your property with prostitutes comes home, you kill the fattened calf for him!" (Luke 15:30).

Back in the sixties, when masses of street people came to Christ and into the church, people made such a fuss over them as they gave their testimonies and sang their weird music. Meanwhile, good little church kids who had always obeyed and stayed close to home watched with resentment. No one had ever killed the fattened calf for them!

How very difficult the fattened calf can be. There is another story that illustrates this. A woman I met at a conference told me how she was sexually abused as a small child by her father. She grew up, overcame the emotional damage that had been done, and eventually married a missionary. Years later, after her children were fully grown, she received a letter from her father telling her he had become a Christian and had asked God for forgiveness and received it. He had, moreover, realized he had sinned dreadfully against her, and was writing to ask for her pardon.

Feelings she didn't know were there suddenly surfaced. It wasn't fair! He should pay for what he had done, she thought bitterly. It was all too easy. And now he was going to be part of the family! She was sure her home church was busy killing the fattened calf for him and that she would be invited to the party! She was angry, resentful, and determined "she would not go in."

Then she had a dream. She saw her father standing on an empty stage. Above him appeared the hands of God holding a white robe of righteousness. She recognized it at once, for she was wearing one just like it! As the robe began to descend toward her father, she woke up crying out, "No! It isn't fair! What about me?"

The only way she could finally rejoice, as her heavenly Father pleaded with her to do, was to realize that her earthly father was now wearing the same robe that she was. They were the same in God's sight. It had cost his Son's life to provide both those robes. As she began to see her father clothed with the garments of grace, she was able to begin to rejoice.

The fact is, we brothers and sisters in Christ need each other. If we wear the same robe, we must learn to work together for the Father's sake. There are people in the far country who need us—people still mired in the muck of the pigsty. They are waiting to hear the Good News. If we can unite our hearts as we share the Father's inheritance, then we are well on the way to delighting his heart. He loves to look down from heaven and see loving harmony between his own.

My mother used to say that when she was gone she wanted only one thing from my sister and me. She wanted to know we would keep in touch and work on our relationship. I never really understood why she felt so strongly about it until I had my own three children. Now they are adults and I, too, work hard at promoting harmony and understanding among them. History repeats itself as I ask them to continue working on loving each other after I am no longer here.

Both of the prodigal sons (yes, there were really two) were running on empty! Both had wandered away. Yet the love of their father never wavered. And the same is true for us. The Father is waiting with open arms. His Son died for all prodigals, and he and his angels rejoice when each one returns home to him. And he wants us to rejoice together when that happens. That's when he sees that Jesus' death, the travail of his soul, is satisfied.

> Forgiveness has great vision,
>   sharpened by stern exercise.
> Daily He's found scanning hope's horizon,
>   willing a dear, familiar figure into sight.
>
> And when at last He sees His son,
>   limping toward home,
> Forgiveness doesn't grab a bullhorn and
>   start yelling orders—
> "Down on your knees, boy,
>   you'll pay for the pain

you've caused
your brother and me—
   grovel first—grace next."

Forgiveness knows full well that the
   penitent's purse is a barren wallet of want
      unable to birth payment
         for past sin.

Crushed against his Father's heart,
   salt on his lips—the child
   lays down the works of grief at his Father's
   feet—
"I'm sorry, Dad—I'm so sorry,
   I was so wrong."

Joy in heaven! Angels' laughter
   wakes the birds at midnight,
      sure that it is dawn!

The Father digs a deep grave for
   the past and
   leaves the death of love behind.

The present waits—
   January transfigured
      by apple blossom—
         miracle of life!

Dressed for the feast,
   the fatted calf
      awaits
         the celebration.
THE MASTER'S SON IS HOME!

Refueling

1. Read Luke 15:11-24 and find the verses that correspond with each stanza in the above poem on forgiveness. What stanza do you like best, and why?

2. Why doesn't the Father run after us? If you've ever lived in "the far country," what one thing would you warn people about? Review the steps we need to take to come "home."

3. Circle one of these words and write a brief note to the Father about it (it can be a "please," "sorry," or "thank-you" note.):
   - (a) robe
   - (b) ring
   - (c) shoes

4. Read Luke 15:25-32. What do you enjoy about the Father's presence? Can you identify with the older brother? How?

5. Do you enjoy the Father's family, your fellow Christians? Be honest. Why? Why not? What does the Father say about his family? See Ephesians 4:2-7, 15-16, 25-27, and 29-32.

Prayer Time

Pray for prodigals you know who are in the pigsty—and prodigals in the pew, also—that all will come home to God.

7

Martha

Busyness

As Jesus and his disciples were on their way, he came to a village where a woman named Martha opened her home to him. She had a sister called Mary, who sat at the Lord's feet listening to what he said. But Martha was distracted by all the preparations that had to be made. She came to him and asked, "Lord, don't you care that my sister has left me to do the work by myself? Tell her to help me!"

"Martha, Martha," the Lord answered, "you are worried and upset about many things, but only one thing is needed. Mary has chosen what is better, and it will not be taken away from her."

Luke 10:38-42

*T*here was no question about it. Martha was not afraid of hard work!

Jesus and his disciples were coming to town. That meant there would be at least thirteen hungry men for dinner. And since several women often accompanied Jesus on his tours of ministry, that possibly meant four or five more to cater for (Luke 8:1-3). And there were bound to be the hangers-on: perhaps a couple of cleansed lepers (she'd make sure they'd been to the priests to be thoroughly checked out before she let them join her guests), a tax collector or two, some disreputable vagabond, and who knew who else!

Jesus was always welcome in Martha's home, and it seems likely that he frequently visited with Martha and her sister Mary and her brother Lazarus. And we definitely get the impression that Martha was not afraid of the hard work involved in serving her guests.

I came to the conclusion years ago that some women in the church are Marthas by nature and some are Marys. The Marthas are practical: they love to serve. The Marys are the mystical dreamers: they love to pray. No one is purely one or the other, of course, because of the way our personalities are designed, but most of us tend to lean toward one or the other.

My mother-in-law was a Martha by nature. We used to tease her that she polished the very pebbles on the path leading to her house! She told me that the secret of good housekeeping was that everything had a place. And in her incredibly well-kept house, indeed it did. (Everything in my house had a place too, but I could never remember quite where it was!) Mother Briscoe was a Martha all right, but just occasionally we would find her polishing a pair of shoes as if she had some personal vendetta against them. Yes, there were times when even she didn't altogether enjoy being a Martha.

Work is a part of life as God intended it to be. But when our work becomes a snare to us, it's time to sit back and listen to what Jesus says about it.

The Lord certainly appreciates those who work hard. He considered work important enough to make it a part of Paradise. "The Lord God took the man and put him in the Garden of Eden to work it and take care of it" (Gen. 2:15). Work had its place even right in the middle of the Garden of Eden!

God worked hard himself, too. After all, he was pretty busy during those days of creation. He didn't stop for cups of tea (which he definitely would have done had he been English), or a midday snooze (which he would have indulged in had he been Italian), or even to watch the California Angels play (which he would certainly have done had he been American)! He didn't, in fact, stop at all until he was through. But after God had finished his work, he did stop for a rest—and he expects us to do the same. There is a busyness that is blessed and there is a busyness that isn't!

God thought work was so important that he used up one of his Ten Commandments to deal with it. The Ten Commandments, as someone has said, are not Ten Suggestions! They are God's mandate for all people. Sin didn't change God's mind about work—it just made it necessary for him to command us to get it done, how to go about it, and when to stop.

"Six days you shall labor and do all your work," says the Scripture (Exod. 20:8). Notice it says, all your work—not some of your work, not just the work you like doing (there will always be thistles!), not even the work you feel you are being properly remunerated for. It says all your work.

We live in a world where it is assumed that the only work worth doing is work for which we are monetarily rewarded. But just think how much work you do that is not rewarded by money—and how worthwhile it is. Have your children ever given you a paycheck at the end of a busy week and said, "Well done, Mom. Good job. And we put in some extra for the overtime you spent with us Tuesday"? Of course not. For this kind of work, we receive another kind of reward. What money can buy an "I love you, Mom" at the end of the day? And for our Christian service we are paid in heavenly currency. I'm sure Adam and Eve never saw a dollar bill in the Garden of Eden, either! Yet God intended their labor to be rewarding and fruitful.

There is joy in doing God's will. As the lovely old prayer of St. Ignatius of Loyola suggests:

> Teach us, Good Lord, to serve Thee as Thou deservest:
> To give and not to count the cost
> To fight and not to heed the wounds
> To toil and not to seek for rest
> To labor and not to ask for any reward
> Save the joy of knowing
> That we do Thy will!

Now I don't mean for a minute that we should not get paid for an honest day's work or for full-time ministry; but I do wonder about looking for reward before we ever volunteer. Some of us won't put ourselves out unless we are guaranteed cash, applause, recognition, or status—all things that boost our egos and stroke our ambitious natures. An awful lot of busyness that passes for charity is only a bid for a "place in the sun"—a spiritual or political ploy to make us look good or feel good, or even to appease a guilty conscience. If this is the case, our work and the busyness associated with it may leave us throwing a Martha-like tantrum.

Martha was looking for a reward! She wanted Jesus to notice all her efforts and thank her for them. He noticed all right—and he rebuked her. Why? Well, basically because Martha was busy doing work the Lord had not asked her to do and didn't want her to do—and, therefore, work he didn't appreciate. He knew there were more important things to be done at that moment, and he wanted her to concentrate on those. By overdoing that which didn't need doing, Martha had no time or energy left for the more important task.

Those of us with Martha natures usually overdo until we are done in. We are bound to get irritable, unhappy, and exhausted if we insist on doing things without any reference to Christ. No matter how much we love doing our work, we have no right to love doing it if he wants us to be doing something else!

What sort of work are we talking about? The Bible says Martha was busy with "much" serving (KJV). The NIV renders it, "by *all* the preparations that had to be made." (Luke 10:40). Now there was no doubt about it, preparations had to be made: beds don't make themselves, food doesn't prepare itself, and tables don't set themselves. In Martha's case, water didn't draw itself out of the well, dough didn't knead itself into bread, and the water basins for washing dirty feet didn't materialize out of nowhere.

Preparations had to be made. The question was, how many? Jesus talked of "many dishes, when one dish would do." Did Martha need to prepare five courses or one? Perhaps she was famous for her culinary expertise and her pride wouldn't allow her to serve her guests less than a banquet. But Martha needed to learn the art of leaving things undone. It wasn't a question of good or bad, but better and best. Jesus said, "Mary has chosen what is better" (Luke 10:42). He was talking about prioritizing our priorities!

However, we must be careful also to notice the Lord's tender treatment of his harassed hostess. "Martha, Martha," he began, using her name twice to soften his rebuke. And he acknowledged her work on his behalf. Jesus realized that Martha undoubtedly believed she was serving him exactly as he wished to be served. She was working for him just as hard as she knew how, and the Lord wanted her to know he had indeed noticed and appreciated all her thoughtful plans. But he also wanted her to see things clearly for what they were.

Martha was not only a wonderful worker—she was a wonderful worrier! "You are worried and upset about many things," Jesus remarked (Luke 10:41). As with Martha, we get upset and worried when we have allowed our legitimate service to become distracting. And when our very activity distracts us from the One we serve, we are in deep trouble. How do we know when we are letting our service distract us? By our anxiety and our attitude.

Martha worried about good things like hospitality, and about serving God and the Lord Jesus. She undoubtedly worried about whether the disciples were getting their clothes washed properly, and I'm sure she was constantly concerned about whether her ailing brother Lazarus was taking his medicine. She probably worried about her sister Mary, who was always so impractical and dreamy. And if there was nothing left to worry about, Martha would invent something. She *needed* to be told that all this worrying, even her worrying about serving the Lord, was actually distracting her from him.

I can truly identify with Martha, for I am by nature a worrier. I worry about everything. In fact, it isn't a normal day unless I've had a good worry. The fact that I worry, worries me, of course, but the only thing that stops me is to know that God worries about me worrying!

He knows about the destructive distraction of worry. I can't serve him if I'm worrying. What's more, worry compels me to be busier than ever because it has me worrying that I'm not busy enough! Worry disrupts. It plays absolute havoc with our relationships. Worry makes us worry about people who don't worry!

Look at Martha's words to *Jesus*. "Lord, don't you *care?*" she cried. And her comments about Mary sound downright petulant. "My sister has left me to do the work by myself!" It takes a lot of energy to worry for everyone else around you who isn't worrying.

Martha was frustrated and upset because both Jesus and Mary were not as worried and upset as she was! Their obvious enjoyment of the time they were spending together irritated Martha to no end. Can't you just hear her saying, "Well, I'd just love to sit at Jesus' feet too, but *someone* has to do the work!" There is a lot more than worry underneath statements like that, isn't there?

"Martha, Martha, only one thing is needed," Jesus said. Yes, there are things that have to be done, and if we don't tackle them, they are likely to be left undone. But in doing all this, have we left undone the one thing that really needs to be done?

Jesus said we mustn't worry about things that must be done. That worry is, in the end, a lack of trust in our heavenly Father, who knows all our needs and has promised to meet them. (In another place he told us to look at the birds and realize that our feathered friends don't worry at all and yet are wonderfully cared for.) When we are trying to prioritize our priorities, we should remember Jesus' point: There are many things we should do, but there is *one* thing we *must* do, and that is to put him first, at the very top of the list of "things I should do today." We must make sure we meet with him, and that meeting is called "worship." If we don't do this, we will soon be running on empty!

Jesus used Mary as a model for Martha at this point. "Mary has chosen what is better," he explained. She met with him, spent time with him.

We have a choice here (we always do). We can worry or we can worship! Strangely enough, busy people find it a whole lot easier to worry than to worship. When we worry, we feel we are still in control, even if we are worrying about things out of our control. At least we feel we are doing something about the situation. We are worrying!

When we worship, however, we ask God to take control and we let him do the worrying for us. He is concerned for us with a deep anxiety, a deep concern. The problem is—Marthas like to be in control! Notice, Martha didn't say to Mary, "You take over and tell *me* what to do." No, she wanted Mary to help her. She wanted to stay firmly in control. It's hard to give control up to someone else. Worship says, "Dear Lord, you are quite capable of controlling this situation. I should have asked you what you would like to eat, not provided seven courses you might not even want. You are the Lord; I am the servant—direct me."

When we worship, I have observed, we are not only able to give up control, but we find God helps us not to worry about what others say about us when we do! I can't help wondering if Martha was anxious not to tarnish her "image." I'm quite sure she had a wonderful reputation as a hostess with the mostest! What would everyone say if she only provided tea and toast and told everyone to help themselves? And since women were men's servants in her culture, wouldn't the men have been flabbergasted to find the two sisters sitting at Jesus' feet, being taught by him, rather than scurrying around to make them comfortable?

After all, in spite of the Lord's example of treating women with dignity and respect, most of the disciples were typical Jewish men of their day and were accustomed to praying a daily prayer that went something like this: "I thank Thee God I am not a slave, I am not a Gentile, I am not a woman!"

Worship helps us care more about what he thinks of us than what others think! Spending time with Christ focuses our attention on what and Who is important.

Martha saw Mary as lazy, thoughtless, unkind, and out of her place. Jesus saw Mary as obedient, thoughtful, and kind; he saw her busy putting first things first. Worship helps us see Mary with new eyes. His eyes!

In the King James Version, Luke 10:39 reads, "And [Martha] had a sister called Mary, which *also* sat at Jesus' feet. . . ." It seems evident from this that Martha *did* worship Jesus; she just did it in a shorter length of time than her sister. Which brings us to another point: How long should we sit at Jesus' feet and listen to his Word? Is there a certain number of minutes that makes the magic difference? I don't believe so. I just believe that, like Mary, we need to sit there long enough to make the difference.

What difference? The difference between being a sour servant and a sweet servant. Enough time for Christ to change us from a restless, fretful person into a trustful, peaceful one. Enough time to see ourselves as he sees us. Sometimes that transformation may take five minutes; sometimes it may take fifty-five! All I am saying is that we need to stay still long enough for Christ to fill our agitated hearts with his peace that "passes all understanding" (Phil. 4:7, KJV).

I wrote the following poem after one such Mary time:

I'm not a knot Lord, no I'm not.
  Well, not at the moment!
Keep me untied Lord,
    straighten me out.

Get hold of the frayed ends
    hold them securely in place.
Help me lie still in Your
    hands while You tease out
      the tightness.

Tied in tight against myself
    twisted over in
      knots of notness
I'm no good to You or me
    or the people I love!

    Help me Lord
      not to be a knot!

Stay at Jesus' feet until you see the world through his eyes. Jesus knew the people with him were there because of him, not because of Martha! They would be delighted to see dear Martha, of course, and no doubt be doubly delighted to eat her food and enjoy her lovely home. But in the end, it was Jesus they had come to see!

I learned that lesson years ago when I was learning what Christian hospitality was all about. At the time we lived in a tiny house and didn't have much money for entertaining. Yet as we got involved in youth work, I discovered the young people we were working with were very eager to come into our home, whereas they were extremely uncomfortable in a church. They were not interested in the color of the drapes or the way a meal was served, but they loved being included in our family. They loved just "hanging around," whether I was ironing, or bathing the baby, or sewing buttons on a child's coat.

One of the boys gave me a clue as to the attraction when one day he remarked rather wistfully, "Jesus lives in this 'ere house. Wish he lived in mine!" That was it then. They had come because of him—not because of me!

Today as there are fewer and fewer intact homes and more and more out-of-tact kids (and adults), we need to realize what a privilege we have to be Marthas in the right sense—to simply open up our homes and create a comfortable and happy environment where a relationship with Christ can develop. After we have done that, we can then be Marys—showing our guests how important it is to make sure Jesus is the first one to be served in our lives and in our families.

How do we do all this—without worrying about it, of course? Well, first of all, we need to make God a promise to set aside part of each day for him. Jesus told Martha that Mary had "chosen what is better"; she had chosen to serve him the "best dish." That was Mary's *choice*. If we can come to the point of making that choice, too, then it will help to make Christ a promise about it. Make him a promise in prayer. Then see that you keep it! Someone has said, "Martha ticked and kept time!" When your life sounds like a clock that keeps perfect time, you will need to make a deliberate choice to set aside some of those carefully calculated minutes in your well-ordered day just for God.

Secondly, we need to get organized about that promised time. We need to *listen*. If there is anything that is hard for a Martha to do, it is to listen! Marthas are usually so busy barking orders all day long that the very practice of listening is totally foreign—an unlearned art. To begin, you can think through some "listening" steps.

First, make your body listen. That means getting comfortable so you can forget your physical being. If you have a bad hip or back, don't kneel to pray. You won't be able to stay with Jesus very long if you're hurting; you'll be thinking of all your aches and pains instead of him!

Next, make your mind listen. Read lots of Scripture. A few verses won't do it. Let the Word of God wash over your hurried thoughts, sitting them down and talking to them. Be systematic. Read "around" the verses for the day. If you are in an epistle, and it's only four or five chapters long, read the whole thing. Listening with your mind means concentrating on his Word till you succeed in shutting out other people's words. That takes time and effort.

And finally, make your heart listen. What has God said to you? What is his personal word in your ear? What application must be drawn from what he has said? Ask yourself, "What does he want me to do about this?" or "What does he want me to believe?" or "What does he want me to think?" Don't dare get up before you've figured that out as best you can. It helps to capture that thought in one sentence and write it down, so buy a little notebook and jot down these things.

It's so simple, really. You make a promise to meet him, you keep it, and you get organized! If you are a Martha, you should be able to organize your time with him as efficiently as you organize everybody else's time!

Taking the time you need to really grasp what it is the Lord is saying to you means the difference between knowing the Bible and knowing the Lord of the Bible.

When Lazarus died, Martha was hurt that Jesus had not come and healed him. After all, she and Mary had sent him an urgent message, telling him their brother was very ill. Jesus asked Martha if she believed he was the resurrection and the life. She replied that she did. She stood in front of friends and foe alike and testified that Jesus was able to raise the dead (John 11:24). "Then take away the stone from his grave," said Jesus. "Lord," Martha replied at once, "by this time there is a bad odor, for he has been dead for four days."

That's Martha—ever the practical thinker! But you see, she hadn't applied the truth to her own heart. She had been taught by Jesus enough to believe he was God and he could indeed raise the dead. But she had not stayed still long enough to believe he was *her* God and would raise *her* dead! She could not roll away the stone!

The last glimpse we get of Martha is in John 12, where we read that "Martha served." The occasion was another gathering of Jesus and the disciples; it was in fact a dinner in Jesus' honor given in the house of Simon the Leper. This time, however, Martha received no rebuke from her Lord. Martha was doing what she did best. As was Mary, who offered Jesus her little alabaster box of ointment. The house was filled with the fragrance of Martha's cooking, her gift of practicality, and with the fragrance of Mary's perfume, her gift of praise. Both aromas alerted everyone to the fact that Christ was present.

There are two sorts of believers: those who believe he "could"—like Martha, and those who believe he "would"— like Mary! The difference lies in the choice we make: the choice to serve him first. This choice will certainly not mean we will be any less busy! But our busyness will be Christ-directed, Christ-honoring, and Christ-empowered. We will be running, but never running on empty!

INDWELT

Not only by the words you say,
   not only in your deeds confessed,
But in the most unconscious way is
   Christ expressed.

Is it a beatific smile,
  a holy light upon your brow?
Oh, no! I felt His presence when
  you laughed just now.

For me, 'twas not the truth you taught,
  to you so clear, to me so dim,
But when you came to me,
  you brought a sense of Him.
And from your eyes He beckons me
  and from your lips His love is shed,
Till I lose sight of you
  and see the Christ instead.

Beatrice Cleland

Refueling

1. Circle the word that comes nearest to describing your work:

   boring
   difficult
   mediocre
   marvelous
   tough
   rewarding
   fun

   How you feel about your work?

2. What do the following verses say to you about work?
   - (a) John 9:4
   - (b) 1 Corinthians 3:13
   - (c) Colossians 3:23
   - (d) 1 Thessalonians 5:12
   - (e) 2 Thessalonians 3:10
   - (f) 2 Timothy 3:17

3. What was Martha and Mary's relationship like? Do you think they were very different sorts of people? What difference do you think Christ made in the way they treated one another?

4. Are you a worrier? What one thing do you worry about most?

5. What happens if we take our worries to Christ? Think of personal examples.

6. Fill in this acrostic with the things that make worship a meaningful exercise.

W (e.g., WORK at finding a time for it on your schedule.)
O
R
S
H
I
P

Prayer Time

Pray that the lesson of this chapter will be learned in your life and that the fragrance of his Spirit will be shed around your own particular surroundings to his glory.

8

Moses

People Problems

He asked the Lord, "Why have you brought this trouble on your servant? What have I done to displease you that you put the burden of all these people on me? Did I conceive all these people? Did I give them birth? Why do you tell me to carry them in my arms, as a nurse carries an infant, to the land you promised on oath to their forefathers? Where can I get meat for all these people? They keep wailing to me, 'Give us meat to eat!' I cannot carry all these people by myself; the burden is too heavy for me. If this is how you are going to treat me, put me to death right now—if I have found favor in your eyes— and do not let me face my own ruin."

Numbers 11:11-15

hereas Elijah had been *burned out* in the work of God, Moses had *had it* with the people of God! That's why *he* was running on empty. Even though Moses was physically fit until the very day he met his death (Deut. 34:7), at one point in his life he was so emotionally exhausted that he wanted to die. The people of God were driving him crazy! "I cannot carry all these people by myself. . . . If this is how you are going to treat me, put me to death right now," he said (Num. 11:14-15).

It was not as if Moses had no preparation for his leadership role. From the moment Pharaoh's daughter lifted him out of the river and into her arms, Moses was destined for the throne. This was his palace training—although God intended that training for something infinitely more important.

Everything that goes into making us God's man or God's woman is our palace training. We may not be living with Pharaoh or have the privilege or private tutelage, but whatever our upbringing, it is God's way of getting us ready for the job he has in mind.

Just think of it: Moses learned to be an author in the palace—a skill he would certainly need if he were to write a large chunk of the world's best-selling book. He learned to be a general—a knowledge he would draw upon to fight Pharaoh, the Canaanites, and all the guerrilla groups that would attack his people in their desert wanderings. He was schooled in governing skills—a competency which he would use as Israel's judge and leader. Above all, he would need spiritual knowledge and discernment, which Pharaoh could not provide, but which God made available through Moses' own family during his vital infant years. God saw to it that Moses had the tools to do the job.

I believe God provides a tool kit for us as well. It disturbs me that today so many seem prone to denigrate their past. I recognize that many people have had difficult and traumatic childhoods. Wounds have been inflicted that may take years to heal, and even then scars remain. Yet I can't help thinking about Moses. If he had been living today, he would have had plenty of opportunity to tell us how he was affected by the knowledge that his mother had thrown him to the crocodiles in the Nile! Maybe he would have had a hard time understanding or forgiving her for that—or for his feelings of hostility toward Pharaoh for trying to take his life in the first place, just because he was a baby boy!

That sort of discrimination was nothing, however, compared to the cruel and inhumane things Moses witnessed as a young and privileged prince. To see a whole people—his own people—subjected to such awful treatment by the Egyptians and to be so helpless resulted in the explosion of anger that caused him to murder a man (Exod. 2:11-15)!

And yet, however terrible the trauma, palace training is palace training, and if we can begin to thank God for even those days of molding and preparation, then the healing of the hurts will be swifter, and we will soon be ready to be the deliverer God has delivered us to be.

I have heard some people blame their non-Christian background, a parent's drinking problem, lack of Christian teaching, or wild friends for much of their behavior in the present, and I can understand how tempting it is to do that. I didn't have a Christian background or godly friends myself. Things were pretty secular all my young life, and I saw my share of people self-destructing or being taken by unscrupulous people. But as I look back, I see this as my own personal palace training—a preparation that fortified me and prepared me for a delivering ministry now! Even my secular school gave me many useful skills that I use for the Lord today.

Moses' palace training was tempered by his family life. His parents and sister must have done a wonderful job with Moses in the very short time they had him all to themselves. He was a very small boy when the princess took him away from his parents into the palace, and yet he never forgot his heritage. Above all, when the time came to choose between right and wrong, good and evil— the pleasures of sin or the plan of God—the Scriptures tell us that, "He chose to be mistreated along with the people of God rather than to enjoy the pleasures of sin for a short time" (Heb. 11:25).

Where on earth did Moses learn that the pleasures of sin only last for a short time? Apparently he learned it at the palace! There were certainly plenty of sinful pleasures around him there. And if sin were not pleasurable, then Moses would not have needed to struggle through to that hard place of commitment and choice.

Personal discipline had been built into his life through the influence of his mother and father, obviously, but Moses had also maintained those disciplines all by himself. There are some things Mom and Dad just cannot do for us. We will not be able to make eternal use of our palace training unless our personal training is maintained. The daily time with God when we ask him, "What will you have *me* do?" is essential if we are to do what he has in mind.

But personal training cannot take place in a vacuum, and the workshop that the Lord provides for us is the world in which we live. The palace was God's place to prove Moses' personal commitment, just as the office, the university campus, or the nonbelieving family may be for us. Without the daily challenge of choices between the pleasures of sin and the plan of God, it is unlikely that the foundation of our Christian character will be formed. And in case you are discouraged, just remember—Moses didn't always pass his tests. The Bible records some pretty big failures on his part.

To lose your temper is one thing, but to kill the fellow you're mad at is quite another! Moses got an F for that! He took a forty-year detour at this point in his life. Perhaps you, too, are in the middle of a detour because you have failed a test. Just remember, if you blew it, it is only a detour—you are not done! (When leaders fail, they may need to spend time in the desert before they can resume leadership—a Moses lesson that seems often forgotten today!)

Moses had to come to terms with himself before he could come to terms with people, so he worked in the wilderness and learned to know God and himself better. Then he was ready for the biggest challenge of his life: the people training. And there were to be lots of people to train—about a million and a quarter to be exact! The Lord must have realized Moses needed a lot of preparation and a lot of practice!

God was good to Moses. He met him in his desert, forgave his past failures, and directed him back into use-fulness. Moses had failed with people, so he wanted to get away from them. That's a pretty normal reaction. He needed—so he thought—the quiet life for a while, and since animals were a whole lot easier to cope with than humans, he decided the safest thing to do was find some sheep and wile away his life with them.

It's funny how we can come to terms with our palace training; we can be doing really well with our personal training, but be petrified of our people training! This may necessitate a burning bush experience, as it did for Moses. A burning bush experience is a time to take off our shoes and realize we are standing on holy ground—a time to listen to what God has to say to us. It's at such times we become aware that we are actually standing on the same little piece of geography with God, and he really wants to tell us exactly what is next on his agenda. He is fully aware when we don't want to do it, but insists on giving us the game plan anyway—and the privilege of the chance to play! Yes, most of God's plans have to do with people, with reaching people and teaching people; with sharing God's truth and living it out in front of others in pressure situations on a daily basis.

If we are Christians, we have all been delivered to be deliverers! The Word of God commands us to tell people they are in bondage to sin and that God would love to set them free from that taskmaster. And how many people do you and I know who are in bondage—who are just as much slaves to their taskmaster as the people of Israel were slaves to Pharaoh? How many folk do you and I know who are trying to make bricks without straw, and are groaning and moaning because it's all so futile and yields no returns?

We have been delivered from that sort of lifestyle by Jesus. But we must never forget we are delivered not merely to be delivered, but to be deliverers!

Sometimes this is disappointing work. The people we go to may not want us to deliver them. Moses knew *that* particular scenario (Exod. 2:13-14). Or it can even be dangerous work. We may not be in danger of losing our life as Moses was, but we may be in danger of losing our popularity, our friends, or our job. Yes, a delivering work can be a disappointing work and even a dangerous work. But it is above all a directed work, and that's what helps. To have a sense of God's direction when we are disappointed or in danger is a huge boost to our morale. The inner thrill that God has invited us to cooperate with him takes the worry out of the work. People work is *his* work, and he will show us what to do, and even how to do it. It's when we forget it's God's work that we start running on empty.

Years ago I led a vibrant youth work in the north of England. The young people were mainly unchurched and had lived life without Christ, without God, and without hope. When Stuart and I accepted a call from a church in Wisconsin and began to pack up to leave England and travel to America, I became overly concerned with the welfare of the young people we were leaving behind. While some had matured in Christ, many had only recently come to the faith. If only they would all be mature and grown up in their faith before we had to leave them, I thought. It was a struggle just to think about going. The burden and responsibility weighed me down.

I mentioned this to Stuart, and he simply replied, "You didn't save them—you don't have to keep them!" In other words, it was God's work, not mine! Changing men and women was the work of the Spirit and not dependent upon the doubtful privilege of my constant company. I could safely leave it all in his hands. He had directed me elsewhere.

To realize intellectually that the work we are doing is a God-directed work is one thing; but to do it is another. People look fine from a distance, but when you are forced to live with them in unpleasantly close and somewhat uncomfortable quarters, that's quite another matter!

Moses' people training began in earnest once the children of Israel were standing on the other side of the Red Sea and their water and food were in short supply. To deal with people when they are thrilled to bits with everything is easy enough. But once the chorus of complainers begin to sing their song of woe, it's another matter entirely. The danger of complaining is that it endangers everyone—the complainer and the one being complained about. The complaining attitude can be easily caught! "When I complained my spirit was overwhelmed" (Ps. 77:3, KJV), confessed the psalmist. When our spiritual temperature drops, we tend to lower the temperature of everybody around us.

The bitter spirit of the Israelites was bound to get to Moses eventually—and it did. You've got to be awfully strong to run on a full tank when everyone else around you is running on empty.

"The people complained about their hardships in the hearing of the Lord, and when he heard them his anger was aroused. Then fire from the Lord burned among them and consumed some of the outskirts of the camp" (Num. 11:1). Notwithstanding this experience, they only had to round one more thorn bush and they were complaining again. This time it was about the manna God had miraculously provided for them. "We've lost our appetites," they wailed. "We remember the fish and meat, the ewes, melons, leeks, onions, and garlic we used to eat in Egypt. Now we never see anything but this manna" (11:5-6).

Some commentaries suggest that the Israelites had had no meat while they were in Egypt and were romanticizing their past in Egypt while minimizing its discomforts. So it was a strange complaint that the people brought to Moses and that he took to the Lord. But distance lends enchantment to the view, and when we're running on empty, we're capable of distorting anything!

Complaining is contagious, and before long every family was wailing about the bread. Even Moses caught the disease! Soon he joined the grumblers and began to complain to the Lord. And it was in this context that Moses uttered his death wish (11:15). This was the last straw for Moses. He had had it!

I heard a wonderful tale about a well-known evangelist who had traveled extensively in Africa. He loved the country and the travel, and he wanted his wife to love it too. She, however, hated heat, bugs, and unfamiliar places. She wanted to stay close to home and let her husband do the traveling. The evangelist thought that if only he could get his wife to Victoria Falls, where she could see the magnificent view, with the great statue of David Livingstone gazing over his beloved Africa, she would fall in love with the land just as he had. So he persuaded her to go with him on his next ministry tour.

The trip was a disaster. It was steaming hot, the biggest bugs ever seen seemed to make a beeline for his wife, and she was thoroughly miserable! "Never mind," the evangelist thought. "If I can just get her to Victoria Falls to see the statue of Livingstone, she will surely change her mind!" And so they journeyed on. However, by the time they did arrive at the falls, his wife's mood was set. When they eventually rounded the bend and he led his wife to a place where she could view the statue and the falls, he said to her, "Well dear, there he is, David Livingstone, gazing over his beloved Africa. What do you think he is thinking?" She looked at the frowning statue and replied, "I think he's saying, 'I've *had it* with Africa!'"

By the time Moses had led the people to the middle of the wilderness, he had had it "up to here" with the desert, with Israel, and even with the Lord himself! He began to complain bitterly to God.

Can you identify with Moses? Is the burden of your work too heavy for you? Is it just too much? Are you wondering bitterly, "Why me, Lord?" So often there are too few hands to do so much work. It doesn't seem fair at all. The willing are put upon by the unwilling, and an unfair proportion of God's work ends up being left undone if *we* do not do it!

Moses felt God was being unfair to him. Even death seemed a better option than coping with the continual complaints of these ungrateful people.

God was quick to answer his discouraged servant. When Moses burst out with, "I cannot carry all these people by myself; the burden is too heavy for me," God more or less replied, "I never expected you to! Just as I provided water and food for you, so I have provided the necessary support system to help you bear with all these people."

And what were the resources that God had provided for Moses? This time it wasn't material elements. It was—guess what!—more people! A resource Moses had totally overlooked! When it is people who are causing the problem, it's easy to overlook people. People who are right under our nose, waiting and willing to bear the burden with us if they are asked.

Not *all* the people were causing Moses trouble. There were good men and women among the bad, there were the grateful among the complainers, hard workers among the lazy, cooperative among the uncooperative, supportive among the unsupportive. There were elders with natural gifts of leadership, but their voices had been drowned out by the fretful cries of the rabble.

Some of Moses' problems stemmed, not from the people, but from Moses himself, for he was not finding it easy to delegate responsibility. Some of the heavy burdens that we complain to God about are largely our own fault. The "people work" that grinds us to a halt can be shared, but we won't let go of it. In fact, I have found in my own experience that if I have leaders around me to whom I am not giving responsibility, they will quickly become part of the problem instead of part of the solution! Frustrated leaders, who are not finding an outlet for their gifts, will begin to complain bitterly themselves.

I remember my husband once suggesting that the man who was most vocal about a particular proposal should be given a place on the organizing committee. He accepted the post and soon came to realize how truly complicated the whole thing was. But now his frustrated energies were directed constructively instead of destructively.

God said to Moses, "Bring me seventy of Israel's elders who are known to you as leaders and officials among the people" (Num. 11:16). He told Moses to have these leaders come to the tent of meeting, which Moses had pitched outside the camp. This was the place where God met with Moses and where the cloud, the visible manifestation of God's presence, would descend. The Lord promised Moses he would meet with him and his seventy chosen men at this place. "I will come down and speak with you there, and I will take of the Spirit that is on you and put the Spirit on them. They will help you carry the burden of the people so that you will not have to carry it alone" (11:17).

The leaders of God's people—all leaders—*must* spend time at the tent of meeting with the Lord. They must meet with God, and they must meet with God together. There is a time and place for those who have leadership responsibilities in the kingdom of God to gather together to receive God's special touch on their lives. They need to be renewed and filled by his Spirit so they won't be running on empty!

Once these leaders had been selected and had met with the Lord at the tent of meeting, it was time for Moses to share his burden with them. The people he had been called to lead were crushing him with their problems. We are not told just *how* the seventy elders began to help Moses, but some of it must have had to do with listening to the complaints of the people so that Moses didn't have to do it all by himself.

We have a friend who is an elder in a large church. Concerned that his pastor was feeling very much like Moses, he proposed that the elders, instead of the pastor, make it known to the congregation that they would be available to listen to anyone's complaints. I don't remember how long this lasted, but it wasn't very long. The men were totally overwhelmed by the nature, depth, and extent of the complaints they received! Anyway, at least they tried an experiment in the spirit of Numbers 11. And as a result of this, a committee was formed to create an ongoing support system for their pastor.

Notice some key elements in Moses' team: they were known by Moses to have leadership skills, they were to meet together, and they were to meet together with God. If would-be leaders have not demonstrated a serving spirit or gifts of the Spirit suited to the task, if they are not filled with the Spirit of God, and if they are not bound together in unity in the Lord, then the leadership team is not going to work. If all the leaders are running on empty, it will not take long for them all to grind to a halt together. Gifts, prayer, and the Spirit of God are impossible to duplicate or replace with the substitutes of human personality, organization, and busyness! Leaders are, in the end, totally dependent upon God.

Moses had to be forced to delegate another time, too. The story is found in Exodus 18. This time it was Moses' father-in-law, Jethro, who had asked Moses what on earth he was doing handling everything himself! "The next day Moses took his seat to serve as judge for the people, and they stood around him from morning till evening. When his father-in-law saw all that Moses was doing for the people, he said, 'What is this you are doing for the people? Why do you alone sit as judge, while all these people stand around you from morning till evening?' Moses answered him, 'Because the people come to me to seek God's will. Whenever they have a dispute, it is brought to me, and I decide between parties and inform them of God's decrees and laws.' Moses father-in-law replied, 'What you are doing is not good. You and these people who come to you will only wear yourselves out. The work is too heavy for you; you cannot handle it alone' " (Exod. 18:13-18).

In the next few verses Jethro tells Moses to get organized! He advises him to use discretion and select capable men—"men who fear God, trustworthy men who hate dishonest gain" (Exod. 18:21). Godly character is of primary importance when selecting leaders, even if it's very tempting to choose the clever money man, the high-powered business executive, the popular, well-dressed, charismatic personality. (Of course any of these people can make wonderful candidates for leadership if they are filled with the Spirit and growing in Christian commitment and character.)

Then Jethro advised Moses to make these gifted, godly men leaders "over thousands, hundreds, fifties, and tens," according to their abilities. This was good advice, too. And it is at this point that leadership in the church often falls down. As leaders of leaders, those of us making the choices need to be sure we don't put a person able to cope with ten people over thousands! On the other hand, we are sowing the seeds of complaint and frustration if we put a person able to cope with thousands over ten!

Let me give you an example. Many of our teenagers are bored with church, Sunday school, and Christianity because, frankly, many know more than their Sunday school teachers and are not being trusted or challenged. They have few opportunities to exercise their God-given gifts and talents. I find young people all over the world bursting with potential, who have not been given ten others to teach, when they could well have done so. On the other hand, all of us probably know kids who had a dramatic conversion and were put on a platform in front of thousands of people to sing or speak well before they had a chance to grow a little. Too much responsibility or too little of it can bring trouble when it comes to effective leadership.

"But I am not a leader," some of you may be saying. "What's in all this for me?" Well, there's nothing wrong with being a follower, a faithful member of the group. Perhaps the lesson here for you is: don't be a complaining follower. Serve in your place faithfully, with gratitude for those who have been called to leadership. Support them with your encouragement and your prayers. And if you see a Moses who is discouraged, and ready to utter a death wish, perhaps you can be a Jethro to him and say, "What you are doing is not good. The work is too heavy for you. You cannot handle it alone." Offer your love and service, your prayers, your energies, your time, your gifts and talents. Perhaps, as happened in Exodus 18:24, Moses will listen and take your advice. And maybe he won't. But it bears praying about.

But what if you are a Moses? Well, listen to God. He always has an answer. Maybe you need to camp at the tent of meeting. Take one of your faithful leaders with you to pray, and wait for God's answer to your dilemma. Then you can look around with new eyes at your helpers—the faithful friends who have been doing what they could. Perhaps you have given them responsibility without authority. Now you need to identify who your faithful leaders are, and let the congregation know it. Give them authority, and let them do their work without you looking over their shoulders. You'll still have to deal with the difficult cases, of course (Exod. 18:26). But the burden will be shared, and you will be released, as Moses was, to "teach them of God's decrees and laws" (Exod. 18:20).

Then you'll be free to attend to your own spiritual well-being and to do the things God gave you to do. Jesus himself said he had finished the work the Father had given him to do, and then went home to heaven at the age of thirty-three. He left us to do the rest—but not all by ourselves!

Refueling

---

1. Think of your background as palace training. What one hard thing in your past has equipped you for service in the present?

---

2. Read Numbers 11:11-15.
   - (a) Have you ever felt like Moses? Why?
   - (b) What sort of complaining gets to you? How do you handle it? What helpful hint could you give someone for handling complaining?

---

3. Read Exodus 18:13-23.
   - (a) What factors are involved in the art of delegating?
   - (b) On a scale of 1-10, how are you at delegating?
   - (c) What does this passage teach you?

Prayer Time

Pray for leaders bearing heavy burdens and followers who are not following.

9

Naomi

Loss

So the two women went on until they came to Bethlehem. When they arrived in Bethlehem, the whole town was stirred because of them, and the women exclaimed, "Can this be Naomi?"

"Don't call me Naomi," she told them. "Call me Mara, because the Almighty has made my life very bitter. I went away full, but the Lord has brought me back empty. Why call me Naomi? The Lord has afflicted me; the Almighty has brought misfortune upon me."

So Naomi returned from Moab accompanied by Ruth the Moabitess, her daughter-in-law, arriving in Bethlehem as the barley harvest was beginning.

Ruth 1:19-22

$\mathcal{N}$aomi's life had been full. Now it was empty. She had had a loving husband and two handsome sons. Now they were gone. Life had dealt her one bitter blow after another.

In Naomi's case it was disease and death that wrought havoc with her nearest and dearest. First her husband died, then her two sons. Have you noticed how sometimes one family seems to be subjected to an extra dose of sickness and sadness? Do you ever wonder why? Well, Naomi must surely have wondered as she saw the men she loved die, despite her best efforts to save them.

Because Naomi and her loved ones were living far from their own homes when disaster struck, all this must have been more difficult. A hint of trouble lies in the very names of Naomi's sons—*Mahlon* and *Kilion*, which mean "sickness" and "pining." Since names were often given to describe the character or characteristics of a person, it seems these boys may not have been robust fellows. Maybe their delicate health was a factor in the family leaving Bethlehem when a famine hit the area. Perhaps Naomi and her husband, Elimelech, felt that Moab would have better food and be a healthier place to raise their sons.

In leaving, however, they had forsaken Bethlehem—the promised place of blessing. Did Elimelech and Naomi have their priorities all wrong? It was certainly a risk to take their children so far away from their culture and religion of Israel. The Moabites were people whose gods were anything but godly. Their worship demanded sex orgies and human sacrifices.

The reasons people give for uprooting their family and relocating amaze me. Often it is nothing more than the weather! Perhaps it's cold and snowy where they live and they want to follow the sun. I have witnessed a number of tragedies as families have, without serious foresight, left church, relatives, and friends to "catch the rays" in a warmer spot. Careful thought and prayer need to precede such a move. Especially if the local church has provided a good spiritual experience for the children, and support and fellowship for the family. To remove yourself from a place of blessing can be dangerous unless you have clear guidance.

In Naomi's case, it appears that she and Elimelech left their homeland because of famine. Perhaps they had only intended to stay until the famine had passed, for the Bible says they "went to live for a while" in Moab (Ruth 1:1). They had certainly settled in there, though, for both Mahlon and Kilion married Moabite women—Orpah and Ruth. Within a few years, however, sickness and death claimed Naomi's husband and sons, leaving the three women bereft of income.

Hearing that the famine was over in Bethlehem, Naomi decided to go home, and Ruth and Orpah set out with her. Partway through the journey, Naomi urged the two girls to return to Moab without her. After all, their families were there, and the lot for three impoverished widows in Bethlehem might be rather bleak. Besides, Ruth and Orpah were young and beautiful; there was every possibility that they could marry again if they returned to their homeland. Certainly they wouldn't have much of a chance if they stayed with her.

At this point, Orpah decided to go back to her parents' home, though she parted tearfully from her mother-in-law and her sister-in-law (Ruth 1:14).

Then it was Ruth's turn to decide. What would she do? She had had her share of grief since her young husband passed away, and she was taking a risk by going on to Bethlehem, a land of strangers with their strange God. The

Bible doesn't leave us wondering long what Ruth would do. Her beautiful words of love and commitment have become one of the most quoted passages of the Word of God. "Don't urge me to leave you or to turn back from you. Where you go I will go, and where you stay I will stay. Your people will be my people and your God my God. Where you die I will die, and there I will be buried. May the Lord deal with me, be it ever so severely, if anything but death separates you and me" (Ruth 1:16-17).

Obviously Ruth's relationship with Naomi was too precious for her to walk away from. They needed each other, and she knew she needed Naomi's God, "under whose wings [she had] come to take refuge" (Ruth 2:12). Even though Ruth knew that the decision she was making could mean sacrifice on her part, she entered wholeheartedly into the adventure.

Ruth was a wise woman. It is in companionship that gives itself unselfishly, without looking for returns, that we receive the very things we are looking for ourselves.

A lady I met in a store while shopping once told me she had been divorced for five years. "I've spent a lot of my life being someone's daughter," she told me. "Then I spent a long while being someone else's wife. Next, it was a question of being someone's mother. Now at last I'm through, and I've only myself to please, only myself to think about!" I wondered why her sad face didn't match her happy, though rather forced words, and why she pestered me for information on any friendly singles' groups she could join. "I'm looking for good companionship," she confided rather wistfully. Once the novelty of being alone has worn off, living for only one's self is a very unsatisfactory way to live!

The road to fullness of life is not overcrowded, but there are always people walking in the same direction, and we need to keep our eyes open to somehow hook up with them. True friendship has the humility to recognize the need for others.

On the other hand, true friendship is unselfish by nature and has to practice relinquishment if it is to thrive. We need to hold our friendships "lightly, not tightly," in case we come to a crossroads, as Naomi did, and feel it is in others' best interest to encourage them to walk on alone or off in another direction.

When the time came for our children to leave home for college, I realized I needed to let them go if I was ever to receive them back as adult friends. Relinquishment, I discovered, doesn't mean I let go of the relationship with them—just my dependence on their dependence. That sort of "need to be needed" can become addictive and makes it difficult to make the transition from parent to friend.

Naomi was able to relinquish her dependence on her daughters-in-law's dependence, though it must have been awfully hard to do. But, then, Naomi had apparently built excellent relationships with both the young women when everything was well. Perhaps the secret to that lay in her name, Naomi, which means "pleasure." Before the darkness of death closed in around them all, she must have shared many a happy moment with her sons and their wives.

But Naomi was more than a barrel of laughs! Somehow she had managed to share the Lord with her daughters-in-law as well—enough so that the young women were able to make a choice between Naomi's God and their own. Orpah, reluctantly it seems, turned back to her old beliefs, while Ruth chose Jehovah. Now Naomi must have done a lot of things right to win Ruth to the Lord. And certainly the most solid and lasting foundation for healthy friendships is a shared knowledge and experience of God! It can transcend all barriers, so that mothers and sons, fathers and daughters, and even mothers-in-law and daughters-in-law can live in love and harmony and enjoy each other!

One of the greatest joys of my life is my friendship with our daughter, Judy. We have the privilege of traveling together to speak and lecture and have written three books together. We laugh and cry, giggle and joke about everything. We talk, talk, and talk, until the bewildered people who pick us up at airports say, "You must not have seen each other for a very long time." And we answer rather sheepishly, "Actually, we saw each other just last week." She is my Ruth, and I trust I am her Naomi.

Then I am further blessed by our two sons, who paint my life with sunshine and smiles and make me forget I am over fifty. How rich I am! And I haven't even begun to tell of the love our children's spouses have added to my life. Knowing the Lord is the basis for our love and companionship. He truly helps us transcend all the barriers of age, background, race, and creed.

But I hear some of you ask, "Where do you find a Ruth? I would give my right arm to find a friend like that!" I am tempted to say, "If you would find a Ruth, be a Naomi." However, I am well aware that there are many Naomis out there who have tried to find a Ruth relationship and have not been able to. Or they have offered friendship and been rejected. If this is your case, be prepared to go on alone to Bethlehem. God himself will draw near and go with you. As you travel the long road of emptiness to fullness of life in God, the Holy Spirit will be your promised companion. Make sure the elements of relinquishment and unselfishness and joy are in operation in your relationships, and share the Lord without undue or unfair pressure. Then leave the rest to him!

When we look at Ruth, we see another basis for true friendship: Ruth had a realistic understanding of the differences that would need to be bridged. As the two women neared Bethlehem, Ruth realized even more clearly that Naomi's background was very, very different from hers and that she would need to work hard at understanding those differences and respecting them.

Today we hardly try to reconcile our differences. Incompatibility has become the order of the day—the reason for divorce. But Ruth, recognizing the differences, committed herself to identifying with them and accepting as many as she could. It wasn't a question of saying to Naomi, "You do it my way or I won't play," but rather, "I'll try to do it your way." This sort of commitment would not be easy, but Ruth was determined. She would steadfastly stay with her mother-in-law, and that "stick-with-itness" is what it's all about. That is what it takes if friendship is to turn a bitter woman into a better one.

Naomi was surely running on empty at that point in her life, but Ruth ran alongside her, encouraging her with her promised presence, and in so doing began to make the difference in Naomi's life.

The two women settled back in Bethlehem, poverty-stricken but happy to be home, and Naomi set about to find a way to provide for their survival. It was harvest time when they arrived, and Ruth offered to go and glean in the fields. That could not have been easy for her either—venturing out alone in a strange culture. Yet this beautiful young woman was willing to brave the unknown to fit into her adopted homeland.

God was not inactive on Ruth's and Naomi's behalf, of course. Watching them struggle for bread, he provided it. And as is the Lord's habit, he ends up providing a whole lot more than a loaf! In fact, he had spread the bread with butter and jam by the time he had finished—but then God is like that. Whenever he sees a man or a woman leave the place of bitter emptiness to return to Bethlehem, which means "house of bread," he goes on ahead to prepare a spiritual feast for them.

The love story that follows is wonderful, but we must be careful not to forget Naomi's part in it. This could have been her love story, you see. Boaz was an older man and a relative, and he was Naomi's last chance of marriage and security. Yet when Naomi saw that Boaz loved Ruth, whom he had met while she was gleaning in his fields, she began to work out a way of bringing about their marriage.

The way to fullness is to empty yourself of selfishness! You do this by giving up your rights and embracing your responsibilities. You die to live. You give to get. You relinquish those you love to receive them back again. Naomi stopped thinking of what was best for Naomi and began to think of what was best for Ruth and Boaz! That is the way to happiness.

When our family decided to emigrate to America, I found it desperately difficult to tell my widowed mother. I knew she would never make the journey over the ocean to see us, and I dreaded her reaction. Her immediate response was grief. "How could you leave me?" she asked through her tears. It took her all of ten minutes to wipe her eyes and laugh and say, "Well now, I left my mother and father and moved to England from Scotland, didn't I? Of course you should go! You should be by Stuart's side and not be separated as much as you have been all these years." And then softly, "I'm sorry I was so selfish." She never did come to see us, but I think often of her typical response and am so thankful for the wonderful mother that she was. She was indeed a true Naomi.

Boaz was a near relative of Naomi, a kinsman-redeemer. The Israelites had been instructed by the Lord to care for less fortunate members of their extended families. They were responsible for protecting their interests, marrying widows to provide heirs for a dead brother, and redeeming land a poor relative had sold outside the family out of sheer necessity. They were also charged with the responsibility of redeeming a relative who had been sold into slavery, and were expected to avenge the killing of one of their own. Actually, the word for "avenger" and "kinsman-redeemer" are the very same Hebrew word.

Naomi had a nearer relative than Boaz, however. He declined his rights and responsibilities to claim Naomi, and for his own reasons left the way open for Boaz to redeem both Naomi and Ruth and any property Naomi may have had to sell because of her desperate plight. Boaz was both willing and able to do this.

By acting in this way Boaz gives us the most precious picture of Jesus Christ, our own Kinsman-Redeemer. Jesus, who is called our brother (our kinsman), chose to redeem us from the slavery of sin. He bought us back from poverty and made us his bride.

In the story of Ruth we see God's great redemption played out.

Naomi sent Ruth to Boaz's threshing floor and told her to uncover Boaz's feet. This was a sign that Ruth was asking him to be their kinsman-redeemer. Boaz responded by covering her with the corner of his garment. While this action sounds strange to us, it was an accepted custom of that day (see Ruth 3:4, 9, NIV note).

When Boaz covered Ruth with the corner of his garment, or the "wings" of his cloak, he was reminding her of the God of Israel, "under whose wings you have come to take refuge" (Ruth 2:12). The thought of Jesus spreading the wings of his garment over us, and claiming us for himself that he may provide for us in love, should most certainly begin to fill up those love-lonely places in hearts that have been empty for a long, long time.

Naomi started out as a bitter woman. Ruth met her, loved her, and began to be a friend in need and a friend indeed. Searching to find things in common, the two women walked along the road of discovery together toward Bethlehem. God drew near and walked with them, cleverly and lovingly guiding their steps into the way of peace. They did not see him clearly at first, but they heard his voice, saw his footprints, and seemed to understand that he was working on their behalf as he sent Boaz to them. Now fullness of life was in sight. The wedding bells rang, and Boaz began to provide for them according to his wealth and position.

This love story can be ours, too, for all this is God's intention for us as well. According to his wealth and position, he wishes to provide for us. He wants to fill our arms with good things.

The first time Boaz met Ruth, he sent her home to her mother-in-law with her arms full of grain (Ruth 2:18). This empty-full motif appears over and over throughout this story. The last time we see Boaz and Ruth, he has filled her arms with another priceless gift—the gift of a child (Ruth 4:13). What a joy when Ruth knew the name of her dead husband would be perpetuated. What praise must have filled her heart. They named the baby Obed, which means "worship"—a fitting name and fitting end to a wonderful story!

But what of Naomi? After all, this chapter is about her. Well, we are told, she took little Obed into her empty arms and she became nurse to the child (Ruth 4:16). "See," said the neighbors and friends who gathered, "Naomi has a son!" (Ruth 4:17).

But Naomi had been given more than an armful of baby! She had been given a daughter-in-law who demonstrated her love in such a way that it caused the people around to comment: "Your daughter-in-law loves you and . . . is better to you than seven sons" (Ruth 4:15). And she had been given a son-in-law who welcomed her into his home and cared for her as his own.

Naomi left Bethlehem full and returned empty. But now she was full again, fuller than she had ever been before.

Sometimes we have to go all the way to Moab to learn the hard lessons of life!

Refueling

1. Read Ruth 1.
    (a) What are some of the reasons pleasant lives become broken lives?
    (b) Does suffering make a person more selfish or selfless? Why?

2. Read Ruth 2–4.
    (a) How is Boaz like Jesus? Make a list of your ideas.
    (b) Write down words to describe Naomi after God filled her emptiness.
    (c) What main lesson have you learned?

Prayer Time

Ask the Lord to show you any emptiness in your own life. Ask him to show you ways you can reach out to others who have empty lives.

10

Habakkuk

Suffering

Though the fig tree does not bud
  and there are no grapes on the vines,
though the olive crop fails
  and the fields produce no food,
though there are no sheep in the pen
  and no cattle in the stalls,
yet I will rejoice in the Lord,
  I will be joyful in God my Savior.

The Sovereign Lord is my strength;
  he makes my feet like the feet of a deer,
  he enables me to go on the heights.

Habakkuk 3:17-19

abakkuk wanted to know why bad things happen to good people. He had a lot of questions racing around in his mind, and none of them seemed to be getting answered. I'm sure he felt a little like the small boy who pestered his father with "why" questions.

"Why is the sun yellow, Dad? Why do people's noses stop growing? Why is air white?"

"I don't know, Son," his father replied absentmindedly.

"You don't mind me asking you all these questions, do you, Dad?"

"Of course not," the father replied. "How are you going to learn if you don't ask questions?"

Habakkuk must have experienced the same sense of frustration as that little boy. He desperately needed answers to his questions, but God wasn't answering. Habakkuk wondered if God was even there.

"How long, O Lord, must I call for help, but you do not listen? Or cry out to you, 'Violence!' but you do not save?" he complained (Hab. 1:2). Terrible things were happening in the prophet's life and land. Good King Josiah had been killed in battle, and bad King Jehoiakim was on the throne. "So—why do bad things happen to good people?" he lamented.

A friend of mine discovered her daughter's "live-in" boyfriend was sexually abusing her little grandson. "How long, O Lord, must I call for help, or cry out to you, 'Violence!' but you do not save?" she cried. She began to wonder if God was even there.

If there is no heavenly intervention when we pray and pray, we are tempted to think one of two thoughts: either God isn't there or he doesn't care! And the thought that

God doesn't care can be even worse than the first thought. If God isn't there, then at least he cannot be accused of callousness or sheer indifference to our plight. But if he *is* there and is well aware of what is happening, then doubts are bound to arise concerning his love for us.

Another friend told me she was dealing with some terrible memories of childhood abuse. She had been six years of age when her father and some other men began to sexually abuse her. Now, as a young adult, she was struggling with the thought that God had been standing in the corner watching it all happen with his hands in his pockets! "Why didn't God *do* something?" she asked. "It isn't fair of him to tell us we ought to pray to him and then he ignores our frantic cry for help!"

Unanswered prayer is a big problem indeed. When the human heart cries out, "Is God there? Does he care? It isn't fair!" and there is nothing but silence, the human heart dies a little in despair.

But there is another side to this matter of prayer: What if our prayers do get answered and we don't like the answer? For that's what happened to Habakkuk. After much praying, he began to hear the Lord's voice clearly and he didn't like what he heard one little bit! God in effect leaned out of heaven and said, "If you think what is happening now is tough, Habakkuk, just wait. Just wait till the Chaldeans arrive."

Habakkuk had not bargained for this! The Chaldeans were not among his favorite people. As God confirmed, they were "a ruthless, . . . feared and dreaded people" (Hab. 1:6-7). Now Habakkuk had a whole new set of questions. Why would God use the unholy to punish the holy? It just didn't seem to be the sort of thing that God would do! Not a God of justice and love anyway.

What happens when your intellect is faced with a moral problem in the divine government of the universe to which it can find no solution? Well, it depends on whether or not your name is Habakkuk!

Habakkuk's name meant "to embrace," and God was calling him to live up to his name and embrace what he would need to endure. So the man of God's response was: "I will stand at my watch and station myself on the ramparts," he said. "I will look to see what he will say to me, and what answer I am to give to this complaint" (Hab. 2:1). Habakkuk had quit asking God questions. He had come to the point of embracing God's answers. Even though he wanted God to explain things so that he was perfectly clear about what exactly was going to happen, Habakkuk was able to so embrace God's will that he could submit himself to the secret counsel of God if that was necessary. As a result, God, in effect, decided to answer all sorts of questions for Habakkuk—even questions that the prophet would never have thought of asking!

When we are hearing the Lord confirm the hard things that must happen in our lives, we need to station ourselves on our prayer tower and ask God to help us see things from his perspective. For it is in prayer that we will eventually be treated to a heavenly view of our earthly mess. Prayer is just like a tower—lifting us up and away from the situation and helping us to see things God's way!

The Lord told Habakkuk that the Chaldeans would indeed overrun Israel, relentlessly stealing and squandering the wealth they found there. But he assured Habakkuk that the Chaldeans would eventually be made to drink the Lord's cup of judgment (Hab. 2:12-17). Sin *always* boomerangs on those who play with it.

Along with a vision of the Chaldeans, God gave Habakkuk a vision of himself. This was a bit like our Monday morning mail! We often receive a really nasty letter in that pile of correspondence, but invariably after reading the bad news, we will find a letter of encouragement or a card telling of someone's deep appreciation for our ministry. And interestingly enough, the letters are often referring to the very same subject!

It was a magnificent vision of God that Habakkuk received (Hab. 3:3-11). He saw the Holy One on his throne, a storm cloud surrounding him, and his glory filling the whole earth. All nature was convulsed before him. Over-awed, the prophet's heart filled with fear and amazement. "I heard and my heart pounded, my lips quivered at the sound," he said. "Decay crept into my bones, and my legs trembled" (Hab. 3:16).

Now this reaction was not because Habakkuk had peeked over his prayer tower and had seen the Chaldeans advancing. Habakkuk responded this way because he saw God had come. He was trembling at the sight of the Lord! The presence of the God of glory was far more awe-inspiring than any hosts of earth.

When we learn to tremble in God's presence, we won't be afraid of the Chaldeans when they arrive. And arrive they will. Whether at the start of life or at the end of it, at some point we will awake to hear them galloping down on us. Trouble will come, because trouble is part and parcel of our troubled world. It will take the gates of heaven itself to prevent the Chaldeans from coming any further.

The secret is to take a good hard look at God before the terrible invaders ever arrive. Then, like Habakkuk, we will be able to quietly wait for the day of calamity, knowing the day of calamity will also come on the troublemakers! There *will* be a day, God assured Habakkuk, when "the earth will be filled with the knowledge of the glory of the Lord, as the waters cover the sea" (Hab. 2:14). Until then, Habakkuk must learn how to stay spiritually full so that when the Chaldeans were running all over his living room, he would *not* be running on empty!

How can we prepare for such inevitable trouble in our lives? We can learn *faith*. "The righteous," God explains, "will live by his faith" (Hab. 2:4). They who have faith in the faithful God become faithful themselves!

Faith fills our hearts with knowledge because we in faith read the Bible and believe it. The Bible tells us that justice *will* prevail in the end. Habakkuk was told to believe it and "wait for it" (Hab. 2:3). To wait for the picture to be finished—the tale to be told.

Habakkuk actually would not be around to see the justice of God meted out to the Chaldeans, but he could rest in the confidence that God would triumph, that the righteous would be comforted, and the wicked punished! We can know that, too, and there *is* comfort in that.

I was a very little girl during World War II, but I remember my grandfather listening to the news of the war on the radio when Winston Churchill was speaking to the nation. I could tell from my grandfather's face that something was terribly wrong, and I asked him what it was.

"We are at war with Germany," he said.

"Will we win?" I asked anxiously.

"Yes," he replied immediately.

"How do you know?" I asked, needing reassurance.

"Because they are persecuting the Jews," he answered. "The Jews are God's chosen people, and no one has ever persecuted them and won in the end. It will doubtless be a very long struggle," he added, almost to himself, "but we will finally win."

My grandfather suffered during the war, and he did not live long enough to see the Allies win it. But win they did. And while he lived my grandfather found comfort and assurance in his faith that victory would come.

Trust produces endurance. The man who shows his trust in God by his faithfulness to God will find God faithful in keeping him through troubled times. We can trust him to help us to endure what he leads us to embrace. This is not fatalism, but realism.

Are you faced with a situation you cannot avoid? You can learn to embrace it, believing that God is in control. Realism takes a good hard look at the Chaldeans, recognizes that it's going to be a long hard struggle, and believes that one day wrongs will be righted and justice will prevail—even if we have to wait till heaven to see it. Believe it or not, there is comfort in that!

Of course the time to work on fortifying your faith is before the Chaldeans come knocking at your door! We need to "learn" God in the days before the night comes—to learn what he looks like and what he acts like and what he says. As we use the good times to prepare us for the bad times, we will find faith leads to a resolve to be faithful, joyful, and watchful—whatever happens. Encouraged by a God whom we believe can do *anything*, we can quietly wait for the day of calamity to come, leaving the "Will God do it for me?" to him!

I have a friend named Joanie who lives in heaven now. Well before the Chaldeans arrived in her bedroom, she knew the Lord well. So when the enemy arrived, and she lay dying a painful cancer death, she was well prepared. She had absolutely no doubt that God could do anything, even heal her. But she left the "Will he do it for me?" to him. The day she died, she called me on the phone. I could hardly hear her voice. "Jill, it's me, Joanie," she whispered. "I've called to say good-bye. Tell them (meaning the people I speak to) it's all true! Yes, it is. It's all true—and it's all right!" God didn't heal Joanie, but she was faithful to him and he was faithful to her, and it was indeed all right in the end.

The thing about the providence of God is that you don't see it when you are right in the middle of what he, in his providence, has allowed! You only see it before in faith and after in retrospect. But the providence of God sustains the faithful if faith has been thoroughly learned.

There are some disciplines we can build into our "pre-Chaldean" days that will help sustain us later. First, we must read and study the Bible systematically. Buy a good study Bible (perhaps the New International Version) and begin with the Gospels. Learn all about Jesus Christ and you will get to know more about who God is.

Second, we must pray regularly. Pray about what you read in the Bible, pray about your world, and pray for yourself.

Third, learn how to help others. Serve people. Reach out and help those in trouble. There will be plenty of hurting people to help when the Chaldeans come, and there won't be time to begin to learn how to do it then.

And finally, learn to rejoice in all things now—the good things and the bad, large and small. This will prepare you for rejoicing when the Chaldeans come. That's what Habakkuk did.

"Though the fig tree does not bud," he mused, "yet I will rejoice" (Hab. 3:17-18). One of the worst things that could happen to Israel was that the fig trees wouldn't bud. Because it took years of patient labor to bring fig trees to maturity and invading forces would always chop them down, these trees, when they flourish, have come to symbolize peace and prosperity. The figs themselves were used for medicine (2 Kings 20:7). Only a triumphant faith in Jehovah could help one rejoice when the fig tree didn't bud. Will we be able to rejoice when or if we do not live in peace and security anymore? If we get cancer or Alzheimer's disease? Will our faith help us to rejoice then?

"Though . . . there are no grapes on the vines . . . yet I will rejoice" (Hab. 3:17-18). Grapes were used to produce sugar, wine, and honey. They were also symbolic of the blessing of children. "Thy wife shall be as a fruitful vine by the sides of thine house; thy children like olive plants round about thy table" (Ps. 128:3, KJV), said the psalmist. This doesn't mean the wife was climbing the walls! Rather, the olive plants around the vine symbolized provision and care for parents in their old age.

Can we rejoice in singleness or in childlessness? Will our faith find us full of joy and peace in whatever life brings us, or will we be running on empty?

"Though the olive crop fails," Habakkuk continued (Hab. 3:17). Ah yes, what if we *do* marry and God gifts us with children but the olive crop fails altogether? What happens if our children grow up to reject the God we love and serve? What if they don't "make it" spiritually? What if they are not there in our old age? Can Christian parents rejoice if their children don't attend the same church they do—or worse, don't go to church at all? What happens if they get divorced?

I used to have a horrible fear of our children rejecting God. If I saw them bored in church or couldn't get them to go to church-related events, I would become so obsessed with worry about their spiritual state I would have no room in my heart for joy. There came a point when I said to God, "I don't know if they will ever make it or not, Lord. But I want to tell you that even if they don't, even if the olive crop fails, I will rejoice. I will go on with you whatever they decide to do!" Then there was joy!

I really understand Habakkuk. It seems as if I have waited for the Chaldeans all my life (Perhaps it goes with my Martha-like tendency to worry!). But I have not always waited in faith. Many times I have waited in fear. And fear is torment; it empties life of good things and leaves us ready for despair (1 John 4:18). It is faith that fills the heart with laughter and joy.

What would happen if "the fields produce no food," Habakkuk wondered (Hab. 3:17). He knew they could face famine and starvation when the invaders came. When we see the scenes of horror in famine-stricken lands—the swollen bellies and matchstick arms and legs—we never think it could happen in our land. The shelves at the grocery store are always stocked when we shop, and though the farmers fight for survival in the world market, we always have bread to spare. But what if—? Could we possibly be full in spirit if our stomachs were empty?

"I will rejoice," said Habakkuk determinedly, "though there are no sheep in the pen and no cattle in the stalls" (Hab. 3:17). Sheep produced wool for clothes. Plenty of cattle in the stalls meant horsepower in the fields. What would happen if there were no animals left to do the work, or if the sheep—the lambs of sacrifice—were stolen away by the invader?

There was one particular sheep that every peasant family nurtured in a very special way. The mother of the household would tuck the animal securely underneath her arm while she went about her daily work. With one hand under its jaw she would keep its mouth working. With the other hand she would stuff it with mulberry leaves—fattening it until it was plump and tender.

Don't we tenderly fatten the little lambs in our Sunday schools and Bible studies in this fashion? We stuff their mouths full all the time—even helping them to chew their food! But when we look for some self-sacrifice from our specially pampered flock, we all too often find no sheep in the pen. They are gone! Can we rejoice when we have poured our lives into a child or a fellow Christian and there is no return for all the hours of nursing and nurturing? Then again, what if there is no one to do the donkey work for us? How often I have found myself running on empty because I was once more left to "do it all," or so it seemed!

Habakkuk finished his triumphant statement of faith in such grand fashion that it should inspire all of us. "Yet I will rejoice in the Lord, I will be joyful in God my Savior" (Hab. 3:18). His love for God was not based on what God would give him. Even if God sent him suffering and loss, he was still determined to rejoice. He would certainly not be happy about the situation, but would rejoice in the One who was his Savior, Sovereign, and Strength. How can we ever run on empty if these words are understood and appropriated?

He will be our Savior too, saving us from our fears and phobias. He will be our Sovereign, reminding us that he is God of the big picture and that one day "The earth will be filled with the knowledge of the glory of the Lord, as the waters cover the sea" (Isa. 11:9, KJV). And he will be our Strength, "an *ever-present* help in trouble" (Ps. 46:1). He will provide joyful energy to endure what he has led us to embrace!

Then Habakkuk turned his eyes from the figs and olives, sheep and cattle, to the hills! "The Sovereign Lord is my strength; he makes my feet like the feet of a deer, he enables me to go on the heights" (Hab. 3:19). Habakkuk spoke of a sure-footed ability; a confidence to endure even worse things than had been revealed to him. He began to understand that the low places of life were really the high places! He would know what to do when he stood in chains in front of his enemies. He would strike no bargains with them. He didn't revere God for what he would get out of it; his allegiance was not dependent on dividends. His trust in God was unconditional; his love for God was disinterested in his own welfare. Since God was his chief joy, communion with him was its own reward. "Though . . . yet, though . . . yet, though . . . yet," he sang.

I want to be a Habakkuk! A hearer of whatever message God has for me. If I am to grow more like Jesus, I cannot listen only for the things I want to hear. If I am to have my life fueled by faith and filled with joy, I need to open my ears to his voice and receive whatever word he sends me!

Once I have learned how to do that, I can share his words with others so they too may learn how to have "hinds' feet on high places" (Hab. 3:19, KJV). Then I shall be not only a hearer of the message but a herald of it as well—just as the Lord told Habakkuk to hear so he might herald. "Write down the revelation and make it plain on tablets so that a herald may run with it" (Hab. 2:2).

And there are plenty of people waiting to hear. The woman whose husband has been unfaithful to her. The man thrown out of his job after years of faithful service and a few short weeks before retirement benefits. The young wife who discovers her husband is bisexual and may have given her AIDS. The twelve-year-old sitting in the abortion clinic clutching her schoolbag. These and many more are out there running on empty.

There is so little time before the Chaldeans arrive! Before they do, let's become Habakkuks. Let's be ready to run on as God gives us hinds' feet on high places. After all, he has promised to be our Savior, Sovereign, and Strength!

> Hinds' feet, give me hinds' feet, Lord,
>   like Yours—
>   You are the hind of the morning.
>   Walk with me on the heights,
>   Help me jump—to leap over
>   the crevasses.

You go first—show me how!
    Land me safely on sure ground.
Give me a high view of Scripture,
  of the purposes and promises
      of God.

Give me a vision from the heights
  of the whole panorama
  of Your purposes.
Preserve me from the mountain lion
      that would terrorize me.
Give me fleet feet
  when the lion comes.
   YET AND THOUGH he pounce
     and bring me down,
  help me to bear it well.

Meet me on the other side of sorrow
  in a new place
   in a new race.
In a new age
  on a new page
   of eternal history.

Until then,
  O Heavenly Hind of the morning,
talk to me
   and tell often about the dawn
     of that new day!
Toughen me—tenderly—
  and give me
   HINDS' FEET!

Refueling

1. What do you admire most about Habakkuk?

2. What kind of questions have you asked God that have been answered? What kind have not been answered?

3. Read Habakkuk 3:17-19.
   - (a) What "picture" meant the most to you, and why?
       - fig tree
       - grapes
       - olives
       - fields
       - sheep and cattle
   - (b) Which aspect of verses 18-19 gives you help? Why?

Prayer Time

Begin with some quiet moments during which you "picture" pictures you find helpful in your particular circumstances. Then have short prayers of praise for God's character and prayers for needs of people you know.

Cassettes and Videotapes Available

Sets of audio- and videotaped messages by Jill Briscoe entitled *Running on Empty* are available from:

> Telling the Truth
> Elmbrook Church
> 777 South Barker Road
> Brookfield, WI 53045
>
> 1-800-24-TRUTH
> 1-800-23-TRUTH (in Wisconsin)

Running on Empty audiocassettes (complete set):

> Album #35, includes six tapes

Running on Empty videotapes:

> #1 Hannah: Broken Dreams
>   Naomi: Bitterness
>
> #2 Martha: Busyness
>   Elijah: Burnout
>
> #3 Leah: Rejection